NEWS
FIT TO
PRINT

Published under licence by Brown Dog Books and The Self-Publishing Partnership Ltd, 10b Greenway Farm, Bath Rd, Wick, nr. Bath BS30 5RL, UK

www.selfpublishingpartnership.co.uk

ISBN printed book: 978-1-83952-761-6
ISBN e-book: 978-1-83952-762-3

Cover design by Kevin Rylands
Internal design by Andrew Easton
Typeface Set in 10.5/15 pt Minion Pro

Printed and bound in the UK

This book is printed on FSC® certified paper

NEWS
FIT TO
PRINT

THE BIRTH OF
WAR REPORTING

CHRISTOPHER DODD

BROWN
DOG
BOOKS

Acknowledgements

The story of *News Fit To Print* has been swirling around for more years than I care to remember and bears little resemblance to its original plot. I am deeply grateful to those who offered encouragement, advice and improvements in the story and how to write it. Among them are Göran R Buckhorn, Heather Cupit, Richard Exton, Tim Koch, Farquhar McKay, Bill Miller and Kit Routledge. In particular, Tina Forde Cunningham, Tony Millett and Thomas E Weil applied forensic knowledge of American history, prose and punctuation to my text. Thanks to you all, and to my editor Frances Prior-Reeves and publisher Douglas Walker at Brown Dog Books.

I rowed...

...in my youth and therefore – according to wiseacres – 'I am'. When I exchanged oars for keyboards, three remarkable Americans steered me towards historic waterways where life itself used to be sustained by boats moved by oars. I am eternally grateful to Tom Mendenhall, Thomas E Weil and Bill Miller for sharing their secrets with me.

About the Author

Christopher Dodd is a former *Guardian* journalist, feature writer and rowing correspondent. He has reported from nine Olympic regattas and written a dozen books on rowing history. He is a founder of the River & Rowing Museum in Henley-on-Thames and contributes regularly to ROW-360 magazine and the blog HearTheBoatSing.

Books by Christopher Dodd

The Story of World Rowing

Unto the Tideway Born

Battle of the Blues
(with John Marks)

The Oxford and Cambridge Boat Race

Henley Royal Regatta

Bonnie Brave Boat Rowers

Water Boiling Aft

Pieces of Eight

Boating

Biography

More Power, GB coach Jurgen Grobler
(with Hugh Matheson)

Thor Nilsen, World Rowing's development coach

American Civil War 1862 - The Battlefield of the Bohemians

General George Brinton McClellan
Commander of Army of the Potomac

versus

General Robert Edward Lee
Commander of The Army of Northern Virginia

To Baltimore
Philadelphia
New York
Boston

WASHINGTON
(Union Capital)

Peninsular Campaign

RICHMOND
(Confederacy Capital)

New Jersey

Maryland

Port Royal

ATLANTIC OCEAN

Virginia

North Carolina

South Carolina

Charleston

Savannah

Georgia

Florida

MARYLAND

Baltimore & Ohio RR
To Baltimore

FREDERICK

WASHINGTON

Potomac River

Loudon & Hampshire RR
To Alexandria

LEESBURG

Whites Ford

HAGERSTOWN

Cumberland Valley RR

BOONSBORO

South Mountain

• WILLIAMSPORT

Antietam

Creek

SHARPSBURG

SHEPHERDSTOWN

HARPERS FERRY

Shenandoah Valley

VIRGINIA

Not To Scale

WHO'S WHO IN NEWS FIT TO PRINT

JOURNALISTS AND BOHEMIANS

Bennett, Gordon, publisher of the New York *Herald*

Bulloch, James D, Confederate agent in Liverpool

Byington, A Homer, New York *Tribune*

Clapp, Henry, King of Bohemia, editor of *Saturday Press*

Coffin, Charlie Carleton, night editor of *Boston Journal*

Croffut, William A, New York *Tribune*

Dana, Charles Anderson, managing editor, New York *Tribune*

Evans, John, New York *Tribune*

Gay, Sydney Howard, managing editor, New York *Tribune*

Gilmore, James R, go-between between *Tribune* and White House

Greeley, Horace, publisher of New York *Tribune*

Hill, Adams Sherman, Washington bureau chief, New York *Tribune*

Homer, Winslow, artist for *Harper's Weekly*

Kinney, D J, New York *Tribune*

Love, Henri, artist for *Leslie's Weekly*

Page, Charles A, New York *Tribune*

Paige, Nathaniel, New York *Tribune*

Raymond, Henry, publisher of New York *Times*

Reid, Whitelaw, *Cincinnati Gazette*

Richardson, Albert Deane, New York *Tribune*

Russell, William Howard 'Crimea Bill', London *Times*

Sinclair, Sam, business manager, New York *Tribune*

Sypher, Josiah Rhinehart, New York *Tribune*

Thomson, Mortimer 'Doesticks', New York *Tribune*

Villard, Henry, New York *Herald,* New York *Tribune* and *Chicago Daily Tribune*

Warren, Fitz Henry, New York *Tribune*

Washburn, George, New York *Tribune*

Waud, Alfred R, artist for *Harper's Weekly*

Wilkeson, Samuel, Washington correspondent, New York *Tribune*

Wilkie, Frank, *Chicago Times*

Williams, Forrester, New York *Times*

Wing, Henry Ebenezer, New York *Tribune*

Young, John Russell, managing editor, New York *Tribune*

POLITICIANS & OTHERS

Boyd, Belle, Confederate spy

Davis, Jefferson, president of the Confederacy

Dudley, Thomas, American consul in Liverpool

Eakins, Thomas, artist

Ida 'Godiva', actress

Lincoln, Abraham, president of the Union

Pfaff, Charlie, proprietor of Pfaff's Cave

Phillips, Wendell, anti-slavery orator

Seward, Frances, wife of William Henry Seward, anti-slaver and women's rights campaigner

Seward, William H, secretary of state, Union

Stanton, Edwin M, secretary of war, Union

Tubman, Harriet, Underground Railway operator

MILITARY

Confeds, Southerners, Rebels = forces of the breakaway states forming the Confederacy, with headquarters at Richmond, Virginia

Feds, Union, blue coats = forces of the Union, with headquarters in Washington, Maryland

Army of the Potomac commanders 1862–65

- McDowell, Irvin (May 27–July 25 1861)

- McClellan, George B (July 26 1861–Nov 9 1862)

- Burnside, Ambrose E (Nov 9 1862–Jan 26 1863)

- Hooker, Joseph (Jan 26–June 28 1863)

- Meade, George G (June 28 1863–June 28 1865)

- Grant, Ulysses S (general-in-chief and supported Meade, May 1864–April 1865)

Adams, Charles Francis Junior, Union officer

Babcock, John C, Pinkerton Detective Agency scout

Banks, Nathaniel, Union general

Burnside, Ambrose, Union general and AotP commander 1862–63

Davis, Benjamin Franklin 'Grimes', colonel of Union cavalry

Franklin, William, Union general

Frémont, John Charles, Union general

Gibbon, John, commander of Union's Black Hat Brigade

Grant, Ulysses S, Union general

Halleck, Henry W, commander-in-chief of Union forces

Holmes, Oliver Wendell, Union officer

Hooker, Joseph Fighting', Union general and AotP commander 1863

Jackson, Thomas J 'Stonewall', Confederate general

Key, John J, Major, judge advocate to McClellan

Lee, Robert E, commander of Confederate forces

Longstreet, James, Confederate general

McClellan, George Brinton, Union general and commander of the AotP 1861 and 1862

Mansfield, Joseph, Union general

Meade, George, Union general and AotP commander 1863

Moor, Augustus, Union cavalry officer

Pinkerton, Allan, detective with the Union Army of the Potomac

Pleasonton, Alfred, Union cavalry commander

Pope, John, Union general

Porter, Fitz John, Union general

Sedgwick, John, Union general

Sherman, William Tecumseh, Union general

Sibley, H H, major who invented the Union's Sibley tent

Stuart, James E B 'Jeb', Confederate cavalry commander

Strother, David H, lieutenant-colonel, aide to McClellan

Sumner, Edwin Vose, Union general

Whitman, George Washington, Union officer

Wilson, Union officer, plotter against McClellan

Contents

1
The Young Napoleon

Sunday, 14 September 1862, Turner's Gap, South Mountain
'What troops are those?'

George Washburn swung his field glasses impatiently toward the inquirer, who had cantered up the knoll behind him. Moments later he broke his gaze toward the smoky confusion of South Mountain and turned toward the figure now peering through his lenses.

Washburn froze in his saddle.

There sat the ramrod figure of Major General George Brinton McClellan, commander the Army of the Potomac, known to his officers as Young Napoleon and to his foot soldiers as Little Mac. President Lincoln had lately charged the general to see to the defense of Washington and expel Robert E Lee's Confederate forces from Maryland to its home in Virginia.

The general shook his head as he surveyed the scene across the valley. Flashes of cannon fire and swirls of smoke confronted the infantry on the steep terrain. An endless blue-black column of Federal troops tramped toward the battle line on the heights above, while Fighting Joe Hooker's First Corps marched along the National Road beneath the knoll where the two horsemen sat. A distant regiment of foot burst into *John Brown's Body*, and the next in line took up the refrain.

Washburn, tongue tied, shot glances at McClellan, who remained motionless on his great black horse. Options raced through the reporter's mind. The next few minutes could make or break his assignment from the New York *Tribune* to shadow

McClellan as he repulsed Lee's Army of Northern Virginia, now at large in Maryland and threatening the capital of the Union. Washburn had ridden out from Washington a few days before, clad in dark blue to meld with officers of the Union Army's military attire and equipped with little more than a notepad, mackintosh, toothbrush and blanket on the strength of rumor that McClellan, a general with a reputation for hanging back, was at last moving forward. After day after day of hearsay and conflicting intelligence reports, Washburn had learned only yesterday that Lee's marching orders had fallen into Union hands. If that were true, the commander beside him knew exactly where Lee's forces were to be engaged in battle.

Earlier that summer of 1862, the war department had banned correspondents from going anywhere near the Army of the Potomac. Washburn's dilemma, therefore, was whether to introduce himself or to keep his distance. His quest was to winkle out McClellan's intentions, but his luck in encountering the man himself may hold only so long as McClellan refrained from inquiring Washburn's business.

On the other hand, Washburn knew that some officers promoted their own strategies and ambitions by feeding information to trusted correspondents. McClellan, who enjoyed plenty of enemies in the military and the administration, could be among their number. Rumor had it that some officers close to the Army of the Potomac's headquarters would shun confrontation with Lee in favor of marching on Washington itself to bring about an early resolve to the North-South schism. McClellan was known to be lukewarm towards President Lincoln and the Republicans, an attitude, surmised Washburn, that could be either cause or effect or cause *and* effect of the general's ambition to occupy the

White House himself. For that to happen, though, McClellan had to serve up a victory on the battlefield, something he had failed to do thus far. So he may be inclined to bend the *Tribune*'s ear. Time, then, to put on a friendly face and pry.

As Hooker's marching troops emerged from a thicket to catch sight of their Little Mac, erect on his steed with the stance of Napoleon, they broke into hoarse cheers and tossed their caps, and cheered again when the general raised an arm toward the battle by way of acknowledgment. Seeing wave upon wave of affection, Washburn seized his moment. He took out his notebook and asked the general quietly if he thought Lee was on the run, and if the Army of the Potomac would like to send a message to the readers of the *Tribune*.

'I think we might bite his tail,' McClellan said. 'You can tell your readers that, Mister?'

'Washburn, George Washburn of the *Tribune* at your service, sir.'

'Well, Mr Washburn, bide your time, bide your time,' and he passed the field glasses back to the reporter.

Thus Washburn met the commander of the greatest military force yet assembled in America. In the future he would recall his chance meeting with Young Napoleon as happening in crystallized serenity, in puffs of breeze, whiffs of warm stallion breath, thump of hoof, swish of tail. But on this Sunday in September at Turner's Gap, the reporter and the commander loitered side by side watching smoke and flames and breathing the cloying odor of burning gunpowder to sounds of crunching boots, comradely shouts, screams, bugle calls and gunfire.

By the by, aides galloped up to report to McClellan, who dispatched them briskly on errands. Washburn moved away and focused on the general's expressionless face, dignified by his full dark mustache, as he observed his infantrymen force their way up the slopes across the valley. His horse, the imperious Daniel Webster, exaggerated the commander's square-chested compact frame, a frame constricted inside a tunic that was missing a brass button. Had Little Mac's tailor been stingy with material, or was nature too lavish with its contents?

Washburn penciled brief impressions into his notebook. McClellan was a graduate of the military academy at West Point and a veteran of the Mexican War with a reputation as a strategist and planner. Washburn's brushes in the portals of power in Washington, however, revealed another side to McClellan. His masterful prevarications irritated President Lincoln and Henry W Halleck, the commander-in-chief at the war department. McClellan certainly commanded loyalty from the ranks, but he had been no match for the guile and speed of his Southern opponents, particularly Lee and his comrade General Jackson, known as Stonewall. While Lee savored chance and tossed caution to the winds, McClellan's regiments moved at the snail's pace of their slowest baggage train.

Here on the knoll, Washburn reasoned that the men dying across the valley were caught in an engagement that need not have been fought if the Feds had struck camp to give chase to Lee earlier and eliminate the Rebel threat to Washington.

The reporter rode away confident that his presence was not an issue for the commander of the Army of the Potomac. News of McClellan drubbing Lee would promote the general's reputation and strengthen his case against his military and civilian rivals, not least the president. Here was a man who might have cause to court a friendly scribe.

2

The Rookery

November 1861, New York
George Washburn's first sight of his new employer's citadel was from the sidewalk where the cab had dropped him. Wrapped against the moist November air, he scanned Manhattan's news hub. The edifice of the New York *Times* stood imperious behind its portico on Park Row. Over on Nassau were Currier and Ives, purveyors of artistic prints to America. On the corner of Nassau and Spruce, giant gilt letters atop five stories of begrimed windows proclaimed THE TRIBUNE. His heartbeat quickened at the sight of the renowned *Tribune* proprietor Horace Greeley's nest, known to its staff as the Rookery.

Washburn was fresh off the Boston steamer, his first footfall in New York apart from a fleeting visit to hear Abraham Lincoln speak at the Young Men's Central Republican Union when the westerner was a candidate for the presidency. Notable features of that occasion were the charismatic Greeley's presence on the platform and the vicious snowstorm outside the hall. The size of New York's buildings and the purposeful to and fro of street cars and people awed him. Passers-by paused to glance at the war headlines mounted in glazed cases on the front of the *Tribune* building. He drew in long breaths to ease the anxiety and expectancy mixture constricting his lungs. He was about to drop the scales of justice and pick up a pen, and there was no turning back.

He scooped up his baggage, crossed the street and mounted the *Tribune*'s celebrated circular iron stairway. A sweet pungency of ink, damp paper and sweat swirled to his nostrils. On the third floor he faced an iron door bearing announcement and instruction: EDITORIAL ROOMS OF THE TRIBUNE. RING THE BELL.

Washburn complied. Trepidation and elation rose within him in equal measure – trepidation on entering a world unknown except as an avid reader; elation at escape from the pall of law office and Boston society. Wendell Phillips, the Bostonian orator and emancipation campaigner for whom Washburn had acted as bodyguard, had obliged by opening Greeley's door. Now he must present himself to the paper that he admired for its thought and purveyance of intelligence – in both senses – at a time when the United States was disunited and facing its greatest challenge since breaking its chains with Britain, almost eighty years ago.

Footsteps approached and a face appeared at the grated window. Washburn, feeling shorter than his six feet and doubting his adequacy for this new world, announced his name. An apron-clad figure ushered him into a large room where men pored over galleys of print, muttering to themselves or one another. The gatekeeper led him up an aisle past a man-height stand of named cubbyholes stuffed with manuscripts, books, packages, journals, letters, proof sheets and circulars, past a dozen green-topped ink-spattered desks to a ground-glass partition. Maps festooned the walls above cases of reference works. Dusty volumes of the daily, semi-weekly and weekly editions of the *Tribune* sagged on lecterns beneath windows sooty from a row of gas burners. Signs announced that 'This File MUST Not Be Mutilated'. Washburn found himself at the nerve center of the editorial floor of the most influential newspaper in the land, where editor-in-chief and proprietor Greeley's irascible presence permeated even in his absence.

The figure who motioned him to a chair in an ample, green-carpeted office with a window looking over Union Square introduced himself as Charles Anderson Dana, managing editor. Dana shook hands vigorously before resuming his seat, and immediately took the top sheet from a pile of papers, grasped a pencil and made a mark before impaling it on a spike that stood next to a tray stacked with neatly folded sheets. 'Forgive me, but the tide of copy never ceases,' Dana said, slapping a bell on his desk to summon a messenger, who deposited the contents of the tray into a cylindrical carrier that he dispatched into a vacuum chute to rattle its way to the distant composing room.

Dana, bearded, mustached and crowned with thick brown hair, sat straight-backed in his shirt sleeves, upturned cuffs protruding from his vest. His jacket hung neatly on a hanger behind him. He directed his eyes at Washburn.

'Mr Greeley passed on your letter, Mr Washburn,' he said. 'Welcome to the *Tribune*, and welcome to the Rookery, as the office is somewhat appropriately known. You are just in from Boston?'

'Off the night steamer,' Washburn said. 'I came straight over, thought I ought to present myself right away.'

'A man of the law, eh? I see your citation comes from Mr Wendell Phillips. He speaks well of you. But what brings you to newspapers? I suppose you know that this is a precarious business, especially compared with an attorney's office?'

'Yes, sir, I'm aware of that. I've read the *Tribune* over several years, when we can get to see it in Boston, that is, and I admire its enterprise. It has taught me most of what I know about the Union and the political issues surrounding slavery. I have worked closely with Mr Phillips on lawsuits and speech-making, as well as acting bodyguard when occasion warranted.'

There was an interruption while a messenger delivered a note to Dana, who took its contents in before raising his eyes again to Washburn.

'Well, the *Tribune* has given me comfort, and I'm here now because I'd like to get closer to the ground. Most of my time has been spent in courtrooms, usually remote from the affairs of the nation. But the nation's pulse beats in the press, it seems to me.'

He glanced around the room.

'I confess that I'm somewhat awed by what I sense and see here.' He paused, listening to the muffled rumble of machines far below. Then he said: 'Anyhow, the practice of law has become, frankly, tedious.'

Dana looked him straight in the eye. 'As long as you're aware of the dangers,' he said. 'Since the war began, we have had narrow escapes in the South, where Northern reporters are usually looked upon as spies. There is always the risk of injury when there's a fight. We still have one or two men down there, and it wouldn't surprise me this very hour to receive a telegram announcing an arrest or even a death.'

'I have thought about that, Mr Dana. I am set on it. I hope my commitment will soon compensate for my lack of experience.'

'Well, Mr Washburn, what I am going to do is pitch you in right away. We understand that Washington is to send an amphibious force to Port Royal in the Carolinas to establish a base to enforce the blockade of Confederate ports. A fleet has left Hampton Roads commanded by Captain Du Pont with transports for twelve thousand men commanded by a general by the name of Sherman. If they can take the anchorage at Port Royal, which lies between Charleston and Savannah, the Southern states will be bottled up. I would like you to get down there and tell us about the military situation. You'll need to start as soon as you are settled in your rooms and equipped to travel. Oh,' he said gesturing toward a door opening onto an unoccupied room with a desk heaped with papers, 'and Mr Greeley will be here tomorrow as I understand him, and he would like to shake your hand.'

And with that, Dana took the next letter from his pile and began reading, pencil poised.

'Forgive me, but the presses await, as always. Mr Thomson, our most senior desk editor, will show you round the Rookery and give you an address for lodgings and inform you where you can obtain supplies. He has some tips on surviving in unfriendly territory and sending intelligence back to here. And, most importantly, how you will be paid!'

3
Pfaff's Cave

November 1861, on Broadway

That evening toward nightfall, Washburn was seated at a long table beneath the clatter of hoofs and rumble of wheels on Broadway, a large pewter stein of lager before him and an ear to Mortimer 'Doesticks' Thomson, the desk editor who had been assigned to show him the workings of the Rookery.

Glad for the excuse to get away from his desk, Doesticks spent a pleasant hour conducting the greenhorn round the editorial floor and making brief introductions to those present, putting faces to bylines previously only met in print. Doesticks took him into the proof-reading room where men sat in pairs, one reciting aloud from the original penned copy to a silent scrutinizer bent over a galley proof. He introduced him to the shipping news editor whose team was extracting nuggets from ships' logs and compiling tomorrow's list of sailings and arrivals. He stopped by a couple of reporters' desks, explaining that by five o'clock all the desks adorned with ink wells, paste pots and blotting paper would be occupied by scribes churning out fifty words to a sheet on topics of the day. 'They are paid by space filled,' Doesticks said, 'so the editors are always on the lookout for windbags.'

He led Washburn across the room toward a tin jar of ice water in the corner where a small round man sat at the center of a desk piled high with books, journals and manuscripts. 'Ripley,' Doesticks said. 'Meet George Washburn, Dana's latest recruit to the war. George,' turning to Washburn, 'meet George Ripley, our literary editor and vigilante over the *Trib*'s dignity of language and its use. Don't be fooled by his pleasant demeanor, for he's an eagle-eyed critic of all literary matters. You cross him at your peril if you are careless with words.'

After pleasantries and good wishes, Doesticks continued the tour down below in the massive dungeon where Hoe Lightning's steam-powered revolving drum towered thirty-four feet from the floor, churning out sheets of the weekly edition onto blanks fed in by burly, blue-shirted operatives. Twenty thousand impressions an hour throughout the day, proclaimed Doesticks above the constant underworld rumble of the giant machine. *Twenty thousand an hour!* The fastest press in the world! They watched as printed sheets disgorged into the hands of folders, the best of whom could perform the six folds for each copy at thirty copies a minute.

When Washburn was suitably awestruck, they progressed upstairs to the composing room where the daily dollop of words by the thousand was set by hand, arranged in sticks of type letter by letter, and restored to the case early next morning for the whole process to begin again. They ascended to the Rookery's top floor lair of Mr Craske, whom Doesticks introduced as Charles, the English genius of all things mechanical. As Doesticks explained, Craske's clever invention of a curved stereotype plate cast from a mold of wet papier-mâché enabled Horace Greeley's newspaper to steal a timely two-day march on its rivals when gunfire heralded the fall of Fort Sumter and ignited the war.

'Still trying to refine it,' Craske said, standing before an array of tools and pieces of metal.

Tour of the Rookery complete, Doesticks led Washburn out to Broadway and the gray brick edifice of the Coleman Hotel, where a feint notice announced 'Pfaff's Cave – Steep narrow metal stairway'.

'Welcome to the Bohemians' favorite watering hole,' Doesticks said as he took the spiral.

'The Bohemians being?'

'Battlefield reporters and other misfits, such as yourself.'

'I don't think I qualify. Not yet, anyway.'

'You soon will, my dear George. You soon will.'

Once seated in the vault with food and drink before them, Doesticks picked at slices of *wurst* and reached for breadsticks, whence came his nickname. He introduced a new arrival as Forrester Williams of the *Times*. Williams sank into a chair and immediately launched into an account of how he and Doesticks, on the occasion of the visit to New York by the young heir to England's throne, had spirited the future king away from his stuffy entourage at the Fifth Avenue Hotel to a low bar, where they introduced His Royal Delighted Highness to the joys of the mint julep.

'The prince was excellent company and indiscreet about his tartar of a mother. He'd be a regular here at Pfaff's if his Ma would've let him off from learning kingship,' the *Times* man remarked. 'Apologies, gentlemen, I crash in here and interrupt your conversation. It was only on my mind because the prince was mentioned in the *Times* today.'

'Talk of the devil,' Doesticks said, 'here comes the King of Bohemia.' He motioned toward a flurry at the vault's entrance as a portly figure made his way to the far end of the room and lowered himself into the chair at the head of the table, a position enabling him to survey the company and its comings and goings. 'Make the acquaintance of Henry Clapp Junior, editor of the *Saturday Press*,' Doesticks said loudly, and continued in crescendo: 'A scurrilous sheet, but essential reading to inform oneself of what is not going on in this great city.'

'And to whom do we owe the pleasure?' inquired the King.

'Meet George, what's your name again? Washington? That would be handsome ...'

'Wash*burn*.'

'Washburn. Greeley's latest victim for the Union's greatest paper.'

'Ah! And how is Horace, that self-made man who worships his creator? May we hope against hope that one day he will attend court to answer the charges as stated?'

Doesticks turned to Washburn while inclining his head toward Clapp. 'King Devil-May-Care here is convinced that Greeley and his entourage, including your humble servant and most particularly the redoubtable Mr Charles "Charlie" Anderson Dana, make up the news in order to cast it out into the gutter first. He is also convinced that the *Trib* has never had anybody actually present in Richmond or the Rebel states. In the case of his majesty's *Saturday Press*, of course, such claptrap constitutes the pot calling the kettle black. Clapp has never found his way to Jersey City, let alone set foot in a slave state. Mind, the *Press* may snap like a turtle at the goings on, but news cannot live by snapping alone. Clapp proudly admits that his paper was stopped last year for lack of means, and started again this year for the very same reason!'

Clapp emitted a roar and turned to the fat and genial Pfaff now standing beside him, while Doesticks told Washburn how the cave at 647 Broadway with its low ceiling and wall of hogsheads had, during the past year, become the favorite haunt of the self-styled Bohemian Brigade – the men who stalk the Union armies armed only with pencil and paper, the men who fed the city's dailies and its weekly illustrated papers with the wax and wane of the war.

'Does Greeley ever enter Pfaff's?' inquired Washburn. 'I imagine his presence would amount to a riotous evening? Although I guess publishers would be barred at the door?'

'No need in Horace Greeley's case,' Doesticks said. 'Clapp despises Greeley because Horace disapproves of all philandering that King Clapp tolerates, like tobacco, alcohol, fornication, betting ... Without the benefit of Greeley and with the benefit of Clapp, this vault has become the anvil from which flies the brightest scintillation of the hour.'

And he told how Clapp had adopted his fantasy some years before in Paris when he was infatuated with La Vie Bohème, an infatuation that resonated with actors, musicians, artists and sculptors, engravers and printers and eccentrics of either sex drawn to utopia on Broadway. With the encouragement of the gregarious Clapp, Charles Ignatius Pfaff's restaurant was now frequented by a motley and growing band of scribes who, Doesticks alleged, were generally misunderstood and, indeed, often at odds with wider society.

'No one really knew what Bohemianism was about, but when the war began, the press world recognized the term as, how do you call it, a movement, a movement-according-to-Clapp that lived by its own self-styled art, was profligate with proprietors' money, spat upon Clapp's pet hate, the prim literary gods of Boston,' here he nudged Washburn, 'the ilk of which you will surely be tarnished by the King should you rise above yourself.'

This remark enabled Washburn to put a name to a slightly familiar face on the other side of the table as a member of the ilk. He was Charlie Coffin, the night editor of the Boston *Journal*, whose office Washburn had once visited to plead for a fair hearing for the views of Wendell Phillips, the oratorical emancipator.

The Bohemian, Doesticks continued, scorns the priggish world of Mrs Grundy behind the door of her brownstone, exalts devil-may-care, cultivates wit and women, and affects facial hair, tobacco and outlandish peaked caps.

'A law unto its own, my dear Washburn, an L O R E of its own.'

On a nightly basis, shaggy browed, spherical, jolly Charlie Pfaff directed non-Bohemian customers to other corners of his premises and bade his buxom Saxon girls to keep supplies of his establishment's famous sweetbreads, pancakes, oysters and lager flowing to the long table beneath the low ceiling in the vault. Here the Bohemians – free thinkers, free-lovers, frolickers, brilliant and witty debaters – ate, drank, smoked and caroused. Here and now Pfaff was taking the King of Bohemia's order, and the King remarked that the Queen was expected.

'There's a queen of Bohemia?'

'Sure there's a queen of Bohemia. Her name's Ada,' Forrester Williams said. 'Ada, she on whom Mr Walter Whitman bestowed the title of New Woman.'

'Himself a patron of this establishment,' interjected Doesticks.

Washburn heard a bell chime in his head, echoing an alleged scandal surrounding Ada Somebody in sinful Paris.

'Ada Clare,' Williams continued, 'she who earned Whitman's epithet by entering herself on the passenger list of a steamer from France as "Miss Ada Clare and son". She was crowned Queen of Bohemia for the self-same reason.'

'She, of course, accepted the title with alacrity at this very table,' Doesticks said. 'She proclaimed that, unlike a creature of society, a Bohemian is not a victim of rules and customs. Which is, if I may say so, a perfect summary of the lot of our new breed of letter writer for the press, the battle reporter.'

At this point heads turned to the vault entrance, where Pfaff summoned champagne with one arm and *pfaffed* the Queen to a place at the King's end of the table with his other. Washburn registered a pale face fringed by dark wavy hair parted at the side. A toss of the head threw a forelock back into place to reveal a flash of blue orbs in the lamplight, set apart and topped with level brows. Her nose was delicate and tip-tilted. The face of a woman with a past. While watching the Queen engage with the men seated either side of her, Washburn warmed to the magic of the Bohemians.

Williams read Washburn's face. 'Wait 'til you see the show-stopper,' he said. 'Ida Godiva. She's more mysterious and more talented than Ada, so help me. Nobody knows Ida's real name, not even she, or if she does, she's not sharing it. Nobody knows if she really danced in the chorus at the New Orleans Opera House or ever sang at the scantily-clad uptown bordello known as the Canterbury. She's pretty, she's a melodramatic hit on the stage, and she writes poems ...'

'Although one critic said she is delightfully unhampered by the shackles of talent,' Doesticks interjected.

'Maybe so, but she don't lack other talents. You heard of Mazeppa, the show that's been moving round the country? Where she rides a horse ...'

'... strapped to its back in the buff? Yes, sir, I heard about that. It was playing in Boston but I didn't get to see it. Wish that I had, the papers were full of it.'

'I never saw it either,' Williams said, 'but I know people who couldn't believe their eyes in the dimness of stage light. Anyway, it was sure good enough stunt to admit her to an honorable chair at Charlie Pfaff's establishment!'

The company had risen to twenty or more heads as more Bohemians descended the narrow iron spiral from Broadway. King Clapp now directed all his attention to the Queen, summoning waitresses for *pfannekuchens*, the house's specialty pancakes, and holding a taper to the cigarette that Ada raised to red lips. As she expelled a plume of smoke, Clapp prepared a pipe that he selected from a collection housed in a niche of the wall. Washburn had seldom seen a woman light up in private, let alone in public. Meanwhile, Pfaff was working his way round the table in his most obsequious and attentive manner, offering sauternes and white burgundies from his extensive wine list, and reminding his customers in his thick Teutonic accent that his beers and wines were served cool, thanks to Pfaff's latest installation, an ice house.

Doesticks summoned more lager and a jolly waitress, and assuring Washburn that he could not go wrong with Pfaff's kitchen, ordered a plate of liver and bacon. Williams requested Welsh rarebit 'with a goodly splash of Lea and Perrins,' and Washburn, who had not eaten since his meager breakfast aboard the New York steamer, plumped for beefsteak. Conversation resumed when Williams inquired after reports leaking from the Rookery of tension between Greeley and Dana.

'I'm not sure I should talk about that in the presence of a *Times* man,' Doesticks replied, 'but as we sit in the Bohemian underworld, I will share what I've heard. Trouble arose when Warren, the great gobshite Fitz Henry Warren, reported that Union soldiers had been requested to fire blank cartridges in all their engagements with Southern forces. Next day the *Trib* published another Warren letter in which he alleged that there is no intention to suppress the rebellion. Instead, the people's patience is to be worn out by delay, and the soldiers' spirit is to be wasted in the torpor and inaction of the camp. Then, when the nation is outraged enough, alleges Warren, we are to run after the old harlot of a compromise. That was his actual way of putting it. There is no substance to his story. Lincoln was furious that his biggest supporting sheet had gone into print with Warren's fantasy as the president's armies bore down on Richmond, and Greeley was mad at Dana for allowing it to run. Greeley feels he can't trust his own paper, is what I heard.

'Anyway, that's how it came about that Dana's incantation *Forward to Richmond!* ran every day for a week under the editorial page masthead. It sat above an impetuous call for the national army to occupy Richmond by the twentieth of July to prevent the much-vaunted Rebel Congress from taking place there. As we now know, the army failed, Dana had some sleepless nights, and the affair cost Warren his job.' Doesticks paused. 'By the way, that's how Wilkeson comes to be in Washington.'

Just as the waitress set their food before them, heads turned toward a tall figure filling the gas-lit entrance. He wore a broad-brimmed sombrero, trousers tucked into cowhide boots and an unbleached linen shirt. He raised an arm to the company and proceeded to where Clapp and Ada sat talking. 'Make some space,' he pleaded, 'for Ida's on the way. I just spied her on Bleecker, intent on running an errand.'

Washburn recognized the newcomer from an image that hung in his rooms in Boston, courtesy of Currier and Ives. It was Walt Whitman.

'A stalwart of the Cave since his volume of poems, *Leaves of Grass*, was more or less published from this table,' offered Doesticks. 'A poet who champions sensual pleasures and is himself championed by a dose of Clapp in the *Saturday Press*.'

Some minutes later, Washburn looked up and saw an apparition with cascading blonde ringlets settling between Whitman and Ada, one hand grasping a glass of wine and the other offering a lighted cigarette to her lips. As he couldn't help himself but to survey what little he could see of her figure, the two women turned toward him directly. Ida's gaze lingered longer than Ada's before she turned back to the King, to whom Ada was directing questions and relaying replies to her friend. All this time – fractions of seconds that seemed like the length of Broadway – Whitman sat still and sipped from a small glass of lager.

Again the women glanced in Washburn's direction, now probably in the knowledge that he was a green-round-the-gills *Tribune* man. For a fleeting moment he engaged with the soft eyes of the actress who rode stallions in repertory. A second later the engagement broke as she turned to Whitman while Washburn addressed Doesticks.

'Are Walt and Ida together?' Washburn asked.

'Not in a sensual or biblical sense, as far as we are aware, eh Forrester? But they certainly admire one another.'

'She worships the paper his pen defiles, while he indulges her while desiring to defile her,' said Williams. 'Although he also seems to enjoy the company of the pretty young men to be found in Charlie's saloon out there beyond the cave.'

The three resumed their analysis of the print industry and its players, which was to extend into the small drinking hours. Some time later the corner of Washburn's eye caught Whitman rise, throw back the dregs of his drink and usher Ida toward the exit. When she stood up she glanced Washburn's way, and moments later he felt an urgent tingling as, gliding behind him, she brushed his nape so softly that the sensation could have been but wishful fantasy. The hairs on his neck stood up; he choked in mid-sentence and swiveled round to glimpse a sway of taut derrière as she hitched her skirt to climb the stairs. Shapely legs supported by high-heeled ankle boots receded from sight. From that moment Washburn struggled to concentrate on what his newfound friends had to tell him about the politics and profligacies of the Rookery and other palaces in the neighborhood of Union Square.

When he departed Pfaff's for his lodging, first light was creeping over the East River. Washburn was well fed, well lager-ed and well nourished by anecdote and reputation of those he supped with and those he would work for, with, or against. Greeley, the *Trib* proprietor who believed in the quickest news and the power of opinion; Dana, Greeley's blunt, profane and charming managing editor who ruled the *Trib* with an iron hand and was not afraid to drop his editor-in-chief's abstractions to make way for news; Sam Wilkeson, the chiseled Washington correspondent who knew more of the War Office's secrets than the White House; Sydney Howard Gay, a roman-nosed bewhiskered mature gent who took the Staten Island ferry to the Rookery every day to write Greeley's searing editorials; Albert Deane Richardson and his accounts of Bohemians skylarking in Jefferson City and debating politics, art and metaphysics while awaiting General Frémont's western army to make amends after the disaster of Bull Run.

He'd heard about the *Trib*'s rivals, especially the well paid correspondents of the *Herald* and the *Times*, and William Howard 'Crimea Bill' Russell of the London *Times* whom the King of Bohemia despised on the grounds that an Englishman who rides to Bull Run in a two-horse rig with a saddle-horse and groom, bottles of tea, water, Bordeaux and a flask of brandy, a basket of ham, Bologna sandwiches and a box of Havanas must rank as more Bostonian than the Bostonians.

Doesticks remarked in the King's hearing that Russell's feat constitutes a serious bid to become a Bohemian, though Crimea Bill probably wouldn't admit it. 'Battle scribes who are not of the Brigade grumble their disapproval, but they yearn for the "Bohemian" sobriquet. You, George, have qualified before even setting foot on a battlefield on account of setting Cupid's sparks flying in the cave. Don't deny it, dear boy.'

As he flopped fully clothed on to his bed, Washburn wondered at the good fortune of his entry to the witty and jovial cave dwellers of New York. His mental inventory of a Bohemian battle reporter's requirements for his assignment in Carolina soon turned to dreaming of the slender, shapely, sensual presence who had fired a dart into his soul. But dispatched as he was to an undercover life in enemy territory, there was a fat chance of his dream coming true.

4

Port Royal to Cross Keys

June turning August 1862, Shenandoah Valley
Dana had promised to pitch him cold, and so he did. George Washburn's new employers flung the fledgling out of the Rookery, armed with notepads, pencils, field glasses, a sturdy horse and maps. They dispatched him to Confederate Port Royal to report on the Union occupation and blockade. It would be his introduction to war reporting.

Washburn's first intention was to avoid a two-day ride by securing a berth on a battleship, but his request to the commodore of the fleet was rejected as contrary to naval regulations. He riposted by alleging that it was the wish of Mr Dana that he should sail with the *USS Bienville*. Dropping Dana's name elicited an order to the commodore to give him a berth, but it came too late. The *Bienville* had sailed.

Cantering through the Carolina countryside, Washburn's reflected on how he, an aspiring Brahmin on Boston's Back Bay, came to be riding with the Bohemians, scribbling reports of a conflict that would determine the fate of the young nation. A year ago he was struggling to make the ends of his State Street law practice meet. His time at Harvard Law School had brought him under the influence of Wendell Phillips, the great orator and advocate of emancipation. Although reluctant to embrace abolition, Washburn soon became a supporter of the anti-slavery faction in the school's debating chamber. When tempers frayed on the streets over the Massachusetts authorities' practice of returning fugitive slaves to captivity, he had armed himself with a pistol and volunteered to be a bodyguard for Phillips.

Phillips was not the only influence on the young lawyer. His resolve hardened in 1859 on listening to Harriet Tubman's Fourth of July address to the Massachusetts Anti-Slavery Society. Tubman had changed her name from Araminta Ross when she escaped from captivity in Carolina. She feared no one, earning the nickname 'Moses' because she never lost a passenger on her numerous trips as a guide on the Underground Railway. It was even rumored in Boston that she had assisted John Brown to organize his raid on Harper's Ferry.

When the Anti-Slavery Society's meeting at Tremont Temple stirred up feelings, Washburn took it upon himself to call on the Boston *Journal* to request that Phillips was given a fair hearing. The slender and spry night editor, Charlie Coffin, whom he now knew as a frequenter of Pfaff's when in New York, received him. The office was the reverse of its dapper occupant, consisting of a clutter of battered desks, discarded proofs, stacks of newsprint, bustle and confusion. Washburn marveled at the chaos that gave birth to ordered columns and well-organized coverage of affairs. Coffin promised editorial support for Phillips and the orator's cause. Back on the street, Washburn was lured by the pulse, pace and excitement of the newsroom, so different from the pedestrian proceedings of the law.

He became more and more frustrated as war clouds gathered, frustrated at the impasse of national crisis and losing his interest in practicing law. Every morning he strode to the Athenæum to pore over newspapers, and at eventide he would vent his abhorrence to anyone who would listen at the South's slave-owning ways and their threat to freedom of speech. Even his fellow members of

Union Boat Club were not spared a periodic broadside.

His mind went back to the stultifying life as a boy in Worcester, an attractive colonial town in Massachusetts where his father was a congregational pastor of liberal inclination fated to squirm under the thumb of his deacons. Worcester, like the rest of New England, was under the spell of Calvinist puritans from Scotland, and absence from divine service was a statutory offense. The deacons saw themselves as guardians of morals to the flock, pastor and family included. The Washburn family was required to present itself punctually at two services each Sunday, with Sunday school in between and prayer meetings on Wednesdays.

When it came to college, young Washburn chose Harvard, but the deacons persuaded his father that the welfare of his son's soul would be imperiled if he was taught Latin and Greek by Unitarian professors who didn't believe in a trinitarian God. Thus he entered the strictly Presbyterian Yale. He admitted to himself that he was well taught; his class of '53 contained exceptional talent. But engraved on his heart was the figure '18', being the number of religious exercises required by the college each week. He found relief from religion by joining his boating friends to row on the harbor as often as possible.

Washburn emerged from Yale full of classics, history and moral philosophy, and with the distinction of being elected captain of the Boat Club and rowing stroke seat in his alma mater's first race against Harvard, on Lake Winnipesaukee. He was, somewhat reluctantly, engaged to read for the bar by a law practice back in the community in which he was raised, and he was swept back into Worcester's toxic social whirl, appearing at balls and galas with the most delicate, prettiest beauty of society on his arm.

In the cause of becoming a barrister, he had taken himself

to Boston to attend the trial of Anthony Burns, an escapee from Virginia prosecuted under the heinous Fugitive Slave Act. Looking back, he saw this experience as the turning point in his political education. A storm of protest erupted to try and stop enforcement of the law that would return the accused to his owner. The sight of Boston troops carrying a citizen of Massachusetts along State Street to the harbor to be returned into slavery incensed Washburn. At the end of a remarkable day, nothing could wash the humiliation from his memory. The State of Massachusetts was nothing but a hunting ground for slave owners. The only good thing to come from the case, Washburn told himself at the time, was that for every one man steeped in hatred of slavery, there were now twenty.

It was the drama of that courtroom that spurred young Washburn to enter Harvard Law School, to engage with radicals and advocates of emancipation, and to heed socialist and revolutionary political movements emerging in the burgeoning cities of the young republic. He haunted the reading rooms at the law school and the Athenæum, hungry for New York sheets that dissected the Union's party crisis, and hungry for European papers that recounted continuing turmoil after 1848's rash of revolts on that continent. He immersed himself in the maelstrom of radical ideas brought to America by thousands of refugees who were driven over the ocean by the failure of European states to grasp universal freedom. He followed home-grown utopian communities like the Free Soil Party that wished to bar slavery in new territories, and whose coalitions filled the vacuum left when the old order of Whigs versus Democrats unraveled.

Washburn had also observed the opposing positions struck by the press barons of New York. The *Tribune* of Horace 'Go West,

Young Man' Greeley opposed slavery and supported the emerging Republican Party, while the *Herald* of Gordon Bennett and the *Times* of Henry Raymond were alarmed by the new order. The *Times* suffered paranoia over the New Free Democratic Party and the proliferating socialist-inclined societies of which its editors identified a long list that included the International Society of Fraternal Democrats, the Society of Universal Democracy, the Social Reform Association, the General German Workers' Association and the Communist Club. The *Times* saw the Germans as the most radical émigré groups and alleged that they were 'led by Mr Greeley and their own socialist or Red Republican leaders, joined with the Republican Party with its abolitionist and ultra voices.' The paper also had a comprehensive list of troublesome secret societies in France and Germany that included the Communist Bund of Marx and Engels and echoes of the Chartist movement that had rocked the establishment in Britain. 'Oh for a party of Whigs and Nativists' was the *Times*' constant wish, according to Washburn.

But it was the *Times*' obsession with the evil 'whoreocracy' that intrigued Washburn most, a scandal that compromised the integrity of the mayor, Fernando Wood, and his brittle Democratic coalition in New York. Having turfed the know-nothings out of the city government, Wood and his administration began to fall apart in 1855 when faced by New Republicans, compounded by the *Times*' exposure of a secret society of leading radicals that the paper alleged existed to examine all questions within the scope of human concern, including free love.

The secret society was defended by one Henry Clapp, whom Washburn now recognized as the King of the Bohemians. Clapp alleged that the secret society merely met twice a week for innocuous lectures on a variety of subjects. Washburn particularly recalled one of Clapp's articles, a piece styled as a bout in the ring between two news potentates, Greeley and Raymond. It went something like 'Greeley, the champion of the Republican Party, owing to his superior weight and wind, is likely to win, but is so blind he can't read his own letters and so confused as to have lost his memory. His opponent, however, appears to have some secret objection to winning, probably because if he should gain the Belt he would be in as awkward a position as the man who drew an elephant in a lottery and didn't know what to do with it.'

The reading room at the Boston Athenæum also kept the London *Times,* a paper that brought a different perspective to civil strife in the person of 'Crimea Bill' Russell. The *Times* sent Russell to America to report from the war soon after it began, and his interpretation of the schism was most enlightening, despite the excesses of his baggage as revealed recently by the King of Bohemia in Pfaff's cave. Crimea Bill told his British readers that New Yorkers fiddle while the Union burns; that they marry, attend their favorite theaters, dramatic or devotional, in their very best coats and bonnets; they eat the largest oysters, drink the best wines, and enjoy the many goods the gods provide them, unmoved by the daily announcement that Fort Sumter is evacuated, that the South is arming, and Morrill's tariff on imports to foster industrial growth is ruining the trade of the country. New York would do anything rather than fight, alleged Russell. 'Her delight is to eat her bread and honey, and count her dollars, in peace.'

Washburn's reminiscence moved on to his epiphany in 1860, when on a February night in New York he was among fifteen hundred who turned out in a snowstorm to hear Abe Lincoln, the presidential candidate from out west, address the Young

Men's Central Republican Union. Horace Greeley, the eccentric, irascible, Pickwickian founder and publisher of the *Tribune*, was on the platform, attired in his signature white coat and baggy trousers. To a rousing reception he introduced the craggy westerner as a man of vision who would save the nation.

Lincoln stood tall and set out his stall to the cream of New York's cultural and intellectual society. Will the Southern people be satisfied if the Union surrenders the new territories in the west to them, without conditions? We know they will not. Will it satisfy them, if, in future, we have nothing to do with invasions and insurrections? We know it will not. Wrong as we think slavery is, can we allow it to spread into the national territories, and to overrun us here in these free states?

Lincoln's invocation to 'do our duty to the end' in the faith that 'right makes might' roused his audience to stand and cheer. They tossed their hats and waved their handkerchiefs as, warm of heart, they stepped out into the freezing night.

That's what I want, Washburn realized that evening. To be amongst the sparkling chaos of that *Journal* newsroom that he had visited, to enlighten people of great issues facing this great nation in the pages of a powerful newspaper.

Home in Boston, itchy feet were the cause of his remark to Wendell Phillips that he'd sooner be a scribe than an attorney at law. He didn't mention that Phillips's pretty daughter's interest in him was serving to reduce his interest in her. The more she heard bells, the more he wished to take flight. Matrimony would lock him into Boston's high society, with little room to breathe.

As he rode through Carolina, Washburn reflected that running loose in a Confederate state was not what he had had in mind as preparation for writing about discursive world affairs for *Tribune* readers. He had swallowed hard before confessing to Dana that adventure was not entirely to his taste. He pondered how he would put the advice that Doesticks had offered in the Rookery – about concealing who he was – into practice. You can't rely on US Mail, Doesticks told him, even though it is obliged by law to serve the whole country, because you run the risk of having your letters interfered with. Like the telegraph operators, you can't trust mail men in a blockade. Not in the Southern states. You have to invent an innocent persona that doesn't raise suspicion, like a patent medicine salesman, and write to the *Tribune* in that guise. We'll arrange a box number and a code name so that you can file safely.

On arrival at Port Royal, Washburn soon discovered that Admiral Dupont had already taken the forts and General Sherman had blockaded the islands of the archipelago. He realized why Dana had sent him into the wilds almost before he could divest himself of his coat. He was to chase hares in backwaters and fend for himself, learning his craft and harvesting praise or reprimand for his accounts of minor skirmishes. He must keep a low profile and disguise his true occupation in telegraph offices, where a false move could cost him his freedom. As for obtaining copies of the *Tribune*, forget it. Best not to be seen with a Northern paper, even if such were available. The only possibility of seeing one was a chance meeting with a naval officer in possession of such, albeit days or even weeks old.

And so Washburn the patent medicine representative found a room in a lodging house. He knew nothing of medicine or snake oil save what he read in an advertisement for Rochester Hop Bitters, but figured that he would be unlikely to come across anyone who knew more than himself. The mixture apparently cured every known malady. Moreover, its claims of relieving overeating and overdrinking, indiscretion and dissipation, thin blood and feeble pulse, unsteady nerves and waning faculties, translated easily into code in which to convey Confederate affairs and the Union Navy's deployment of its iron-clad monitors and low-decked mortar boats to the Rookery.

Washburn spent his days composing letters on inconsequential snake oil matters for transformation at the *Trib*, interspersed with private notes to his elders and betters to account for his movements, seek advice or take issue with their briefings. Stories were few and far between; one day he caught sight of a woman who resembled Harriet Tubman, the revolver-toting Underground Railroader. Adams Sherman Hill of the Washington bureau had told Washburn that Tubman was rumored to be scouting and spying for the army in Port Royal, but Washburn never came close enough to her to strike up a conversation. Meanwhile, the abolitionist in him was shocked by the ignorance and backwardness of the so-called 'contrabands', slaves freed from cotton and rice plantations who were living in makeshift camps. He wrote to Dana that if you were not already a convinced abolitionist, the contrabands were not likely to convert you.

As the weeks rolled on he noted his editors' likes and dislikes and, on the rare occasions when he could see a paper, how they adjusted his copy, concluding that his contributions to the *Tribune* were good enough to secure his engagement but not lively enough to stand out on his editor's desk. The war had drawn an army of freewheelers chasing the colors with pencil and paper, their success dependent upon mobility while avoiding the attention of military censors. Washburn decided that he must either make a mark to escape from his backwater or escape from the backwater to make a mark.

Come April of 1862, luck began to run for him when a year-old argument over the *Tribune*'s campaign of May 1861, 'To Richmond Onwards!', came to the boil. The campaign was a fantasy dreamed up by the then Washington correspondent Fitz Henry Warren. It infuriated Horace Greeley and became a running sore between proprietor and his faithful lieutenant of twenty years, Charles A Dana. Greeley was said to have said that he never opened the paper in those days without a terror as to what the headlines might have made him say after eleven o'clock at night. Consequently, Dana's head rolled, to be replaced by Sydney H Gay.

As soon as he heard about this, Washburn wrote to Gay that it was of much consequence to him to visit Boston if he was to be detained in Port Royal for the summer. He figured that after such a visit he might be spared a return to the Carolina of the contrabands, and he figured correctly. One of the new managing editor's first acts was to draw the covert career of a hop bitters representative to a close and assign Washburn to General John C Frémont, whose army was advancing through the mountains of West Virginia toward Tennessee. Washburn was to call into Washington en route to be briefed by Adams Hill, who was the *Tribune*'s ears while Sam Wilkeson, the replacement for the disgraced Warren, was reporting from the Virginia Peninsular.

Washburn departed Washington for Frémont's army well briefed. Hill explained how control of the fertile Shenandoah Valley was vital for Jefferson Davis and his government in Richmond as a plentiful source of food. The valley was also a turnpike to Maryland and Pennsylvania, and ultimately to Abe Lincoln's capital. According to Hill, Lincoln and his general-in-chief, the stout, round-headed Henry 'Old Brains' Halleck, were sending Frémont and two other armies to Shenandoah to trap Stonewall Jackson, whose foot cavalry's forced marches had been a constant irritant to McClellan's labored advance on Richmond. Jackson, a former strategist and artillery professor at the military academy at West Point, had harassed the Union's campaign to a standstill within sight of the Rebel capital, and then turned on his pursuers in the valley.

Frémont, the son of a French dancing master, was an explorer and millionaire mine owner before emerging as a glamorous soldier of fortune in command of the Western Department at the outbreak of war. His exploits included crossing the High Sierras in mid-winter, a jaunt that earned him the moniker 'Pathfinder'. His unsuccessful attempt to run for president on behalf of the new Republican Party in 1856 brought him to Greeley's notice and probably explained, said Hill, why Frémont was favorably disposed to the *Tribune* and the *Tribune* to Frémont.

Hill's parting observation was 'sometimes you don't want to stand out in the crowd'. He advised against the corduroy knickerbockers, buckskin jackets, high-topped boots of top grain leather and broad-brimmed hats popular among some correspondents. Washburn equipped himself with the standard army reporter's kit of field glasses, notebook, blanket, haversack and a .32 Smith & Wesson. He rode into Frémont's camp on a good horse that he had purchased for $130, together with a McClellan saddle, two bridles and two horse blankets, a goodly price for a scarce mount when such animals were in such demand. Expecting to have to account for himself, he sought successfully to gain ready access to officers close to the Pathfinder. He was allowed to read official communications, and the censor left him alone.

Washburn was thus in the right place from where to enlighten readers on another Stonewall feat when Jackson, despite being outnumbered two to one, repelled Frémont's forces at Cross Keys.

On that fateful 8 June, Washburn was in the saddle at dawn. He boasted to Gay later that he saw more of the fighting and knew more about the battle than anyone on the field. When fighting ceased he went everywhere and talked to everyone, reckoning that he was twenty hours on the go and fourteen in the saddle. His account was thorough and reached New York well ahead of his competitors.

While Washburn made his mark as a reporter, Frémont was marked down as a commander. Washburn riled at the injustice of placing the general's troops under General Pope's command. He wrote to Gay opining that Lincoln had gone crazy for removing a commander at the end of a brilliant campaign without a shadow of a charge against him. He pleaded that the *Tribune* comes to Frémont's defense.

Infuriatingly, however, Gay failed to acknowledge several of Washburn's indiscrete letters on the subject. After three months passed, Washburn realized that his train of thought had been rash. Frémont the Pathfinder had, after all, lost an engagement to an inferior force. Later, in the Washington office, he came across a fellow Bohemian's more seasoned account of Cross Keys, and was humbled enough to copy it down as a keepsake. Charles Henry Webb of the *Times* wrote:

'*Some reporters claim Cross Keys as a victory. Feelings and sympathies so influence them that they cannot record faithfully, and will have a long account to settle with history some day. Will not truth and common sense satisfy the popular craving, or is it always necessary to pander to the appetite that demands a victory in all cases, an assurance that the enemy lost at least one more than we?*'

Webb summarized Stonewall's character and abilities succinctly: '*Jackson is equally eminent as a strategist and tactician.*

He handles his army like a whip, making it crack in out of the way corners where you scarcely thought the lash would reach. This retreat of his, if retreat it can be called, has been conducted with marvelous skill. He has not much mercy on his men, but he gets extraordinary marches out of them on very short commons.'

Washburn wished he'd written that.

When Frémont took the inevitable step of resigning his commission, a curt note from Gay instructed Washburn to join General John Pope's army, ten times larger than Frémont's in both size and importance and, warned Gay, frosty toward the press and the *Tribune*. Pope, a dashing figure in the western theater with a large full head of hair, thick black beard and bright eyes, and an anti-slaver to boot, had been called to Washington toward the end of June to take command of the Union armies in northern Virginia. His detractors doubted his ability to lead the Army of Virginia against Lee and Jackson, accusing him of ambition and vanity. Gay passed on Albert Richardson's warning that Pope was a liar, and Nathaniel Paige's opinion that he was a great humbug.

For several weeks, Washburn trod carefully, both to cultivate Pope's staff officers and nurse an ankle that had been severely bruised by a kick from his horse. It would be politic to give generous space to a commander with a name like Pope. This policy was to good effect. He found the general to be good-natured and sufficiently interested in what he wrote to read and correct it. Thus the *Trib* trio in Virginia – Paige and the shorthand writer William A Croffut, neither of whom Washburn had met – consistently outdid the *Herald* with many more men in the field. While inspecting the lines one mid-August day, the Pope beckoned Washburn over as the two of them walked their horses down a lane and told him that Commander-in-Chief Halleck's office was about to issue an order banishing all newspaper correspondents from the lines.

'I'd best pack up and leave this night,' Washburn began, but Pope raised his hand.

'The notification is not yet official, but simply informal advice. You need not comply until the order is served on you officially.'

That evening Washburn moved his kit to a friendly officer's tent and laid low for several days while he completed a letter that contained edicts from Pope that the general wished to see in print, and enabled him to get close to some of the action at the Rappahannock and Manassas, known as the Second Bull Run. When Pope received Halleck's instruction, he summoned the reporter and read it to him.

You will immediately remove from your army all newspaper reporters, it said, *and you will permit no telegrams to be sent over the telegraph lines out of your command except those sent by yourself. You will also suspend the transmission of any mail matter other than that of official communication. Halleck.*

Pope shrugged, and Washburn said he would make himself scarce. He had already received orders from Gay to report to Washington on 21 August and to 'keep as near the army as possible and lose no opportunity of getting news at any expense of trouble or money'.

Washburn had now tested two sides of a reporter's coin, and came to heed his editor's opinion that field correspondents were not always in the best position to determine editorial policy. When he exchanged Washburn the Bostonian barrister for Washburn the New York scribe, his dream was to be planted amongst the power brokers. Now he was assigned to the very nerve center of the war.

His remaining frustration was Ida Godiva. For nine months he had nursed Cupid's dart, and for nine months he had learned nothing to add to her reputation as a naked lady who rode the boards on horseback. He had managed one chance visit to Pfaff's in April when stopping by the Rookery to look up General Frémont's history, but Ida was Godiva-ing in Cincinnati, Dayton Ohio and points west. He had no idea where she dwelled or whose company she kept or where or when she was playing to the gallery. Eventually, desperation drove him to write her via the good offices of Charlie Pfaff. It was the most difficult letter he had ever set out, much harder to compose than the trickiest of dispatches to the *Tribune*. He must have started twenty times, was even tempted to engage a professional writer of sweet nothings such as illiterate soldiers turn to, before he told himself to get a grip. He pushed his pen with trembling hand:

My dear Ida, I was much taken with the angelic aura of your beauty and intelligence which enveloped my perch at the far end of the table when you visited Pfaff's in November. Every day since, I have felt the desire to make your acquaintance if you can see your path again crossing mine. If you find favor with this proposal you may write to me via the New York Tribune office at Union Square or the Washington office on Fourteenth Street and Pennsylvania Avenue, where I nest when not chasing armies. I am, Fair Lady, your obedient servant, George Washburn.

He sealed it in an envelope, addressed it simply 'Ida' via Pfaff's Cave, marked it 'Private', enclosed it in another envelope and mailed it to Charlie Pfaff at his restaurant on Broadway, with a note requesting him to forward it. His invitation had been dispatched while he was sojourned with Pope's army. The mails came and went, but no word had arrived from New York or the theaters out west. Washburn now added despair to the emotions experienced on that night at Pfaff's. His previous romances in Worcester and Boston receded rapidly with the miles he had traveled since joining the *Trib*. But just as he had become an innocent abroad, Ida had set him all aquiver for his journey to Carolina, and all the way back again.

5

The Rumor Mill

August turning September, Willard's Hotel, Washington
When George Washburn arrived in the capital at the end of August, the summer of '62 was going badly for the Union and the White House. General Lee's battalions confounded the Federal armies in the Seven Days Battles and again at the Second Bull Run, sending them scuttling back to Washington to face the specter of invasion.

Anxiety mixed with opportunism made a heady atmosphere in the streets. Ragged veterans of the peninsular campaign contrasted with regiments of volunteers decked out in unblemished uniforms yet to see action. Dozens of the two-wheeled 'avalanches', unsprung field ambulances, choked hospitals with casualties. Disease, and fear of disease, was all about, from typhus and typhoid to malaria and the dreaded diarrhea known to troops as Virginia quickstep. Tented camps grew round the city as the Army of the Potomac re-formed. Wagon trains of victuals, ordnance, battledress and blankets fed arsenals and stores. And at night Washington hummed with remedies for loneliness. Gaudy courtesans lolled in carriages and rode out with cavalry officers on Pennsylvania Avenue. Fallen angels plied temptation in hotels and saloons, while painted Jezebels and daughters of Eve were available in hundreds of bordellos. One notorious example was Hooker's Headquarters, whence Bohemians directed inquirers after the general of that name. Concubines and street-walkers were everywhere from the rough quarters of Fighting Ally and Nigger Hill to the nearby towns of Alexandria and Georgetown.

Gay's instruction to Washburn was to get close to General McClellan as he rebuilt the Army of the Potomac, and to probe the friction between the Young Napoleon and the sage in the White House. Try and infiltrate the intelligence gatherers, Gay had written, a world in which the South appeared to have stolen a march.

There were as many rumors as ladies of ill repute floating round the capital. By day conspiracy, intelligence and intrigue circled the White House, the war department and dozens upon hundreds of door-stepping correspondents. By night speculation on moves and motives in Washington and Richmond flooded the saloon and parlors of the Willard Hotel.

Willard's sumptuous four-story establishment had been at the hub of the war of words ever since newspaper men and warmongers nested there for the great peace conference a year past, when delegates from twenty-one states failed to avert military action. Sam Wilkeson, the *Tribune's* scintillating and sparkling White House watcher who filled the seat vacated by Fitz Warren, was a permanent resident at Willard's, while Adams Hill, Gay's eyes and ears in Washington, lived across the street above the *Tribune* office on fourteenth, and was often to be found stalking the hotel corridors. Willard's was barely three hundred paces from Lincoln's White House and the war department, where Edwin Stanton, the secretary for war, ruled the roost from his office on the second floor of the imposing brick edifice on seventeenth.

Wilkeson's erect gait, chiseled profile and long hair cut a striking figure round the capital, and they adorned more than a reporter. Having learned his trade as editor of the Albany *Evening Journal*, Wilkeson was adept at seeking out forbidden information.

On their first evening together surrounded by cuttings, cartoons and reference works in his office, he told Washburn that he was proud to be labeled a 'fanatical, impertinent revolutionary fellow, who will bear watching' by a rival on the *Herald*.

Wilkeson had just returned from an enforced stay at his farm in upstate New York after his spat with the Rookery over the failure of McClellan's peninsular campaign. He had been in the field for most of its duration.

'Start by reading this,' he said, fishing out a clipping from his well-ordered files. 'It's from the *Chicago Tribune.*' He poured two glasses of wine and fell silent while Washburn read.

The amount of lying that has been sent abroad on the wings of the press and telegraphed to mislead and delude the country is enormous ... all the reasons are assigned but the right one, to account for a stunning disaster. And the crowning deceit of the whole column of falsehoods is to call the affair a 'great strategic movement'. It was just as much a great strategic movement as the battle of Bull's Bluff, and not a whit more.

Washburn looked up expectantly when he finished reading, and Wilkeson described how McClellan escaped criticism at the time, but had come under fire later for remaining aboard the gunboat *Galena* when his army was fighting for its life at a place called Malvern Hill.

'That's the meanest picture that this bloody rebellion has painted so far,' Wilkeson said. 'I wrote a stringent piece which I sent to Gay putting the blame on the administration. Words to the effect,' and he gestured toward his clippings and files, 'that the refusal to give that army ample reinforcement came within a hair's breadth of ruining the nation. I said that I didn't care about the question of this general's fitness to command – a question often debated by legislators, soldiers and politicians – when loyal New York regiments, lifted from their feet by the fire of Rebel brigades, cry out for help. When the choicest of New England and Michigan and Penn troops who are outnumbered by whole divisions of the enemy beg for reinforcements, I say that the blackest crime that power can commit is to stalk upon the field of peril and say, "soldiers, I have no faith in your commander! Let your martyrdom proceed".'

After a pause, during which Washburn emitted a low grunt of agreement, Wilkeson remarked that much to his amazement, the *Tribune* printed his entire dispatch, uncut.

'It must have surprised our proprietors in view of their hostility to McClellan,' he said. 'But they added an editorial note claiming that the *Tribune* was not responsible for my opinions nor my strictures on the government. Not 'til later did it become clear that Mac actually had more men than the Rebels. All the newspaper talk of him being outnumbered two to one is utterly without basis. Equally wrong is the claim that 30,000 troops from the Confed's western army had moved to Richmond. Anyhow, Gay did a typical Gay thing and sent me home on leave until the dust settled at the Rookery. But I stand by my argument. You undermine confidence in your generals at your peril, at least when there's a fight on.'

He paused to catch breath and change the subject.

'It's good to see you, George, my dear sir. Let us go and eat and catch up with one another.'

In a quiet corner of Willard's restaurant over a bloody steak, Wilkeson set out what he saw as the dilemma facing Lee and the government in Richmond. 'If I were Lee,' said he, 'I would be tempted to invade the North to take the initiative against the Army of the Potomac, because the Army of the Potomac is never going to leave me alone, whatever general is in command next week or next month. After all, the Union has hardly a victory to its name since the attack on Fort Sumter opened hostilities, and Abe urgently needs a win, especially if he is toying with declaring emancipation to be a desirable aim of the struggle, as we think he is.

'So if I were President Davis,' he continued, 'I'd be taking the fight to the Union, especially as I have to face a large faction in Richmond whose wish is to be left alone. Besides, if Lee fell back to the Shenandoah or to Richmond to feed his army, he'd give up the fruits of his victories over the Union armies in Virginia. A victory on Northern soil might win some of that European support which the Southern economy thinks it needs so badly, or it might form the basis for a Confederate peace offer in exchange for independence. Even if such an offer were made and rejected, it could win votes for opponents of war in the forthcoming Northern elections.

'There are other factors,' Wilkeson continued. 'We shouldn't forget that all is not roses in the victorious Rebel force. Munitions and victuals are short, desertion and straggling – what they call the wagon dogs – are rife, particularly at the pace Jackson marches his men, many of whom, it is said, go barefoot, deprived of their hobnail brogans. That's why Lee's not going to attack us here in Washington. We've more men under arms and they're better equipped.'

Wilkeson ordered more claret and talk turned to political matters and how, with the possible exception of Lincoln, those surrounding him couldn't see beyond the end of their noses, and what's more, were not bothered by this trait, being only concerned with winning their next election, or securing a post from the winner.

'Take Secretary of State Seward,' Wilkeson said. 'Slightly built with sloping shoulders, a hawk nose and rusty unkempt hair whose terms as a senator and governor of New York led him to seek the presidential nomination for the new Republican Party. Although William Henry Seward supports abolition – he once defined slavery as "an irrepressible conflict between opposing and enduring forces" – he curries political favor by throwing enormously lavish parties where Republicans, liberals and abolitionists rub shoulders with Democrats, slave owners and even reprobates like journalists. He thought he would win in 1860 because of his thirty-year anti-slavery record, but Lincoln had proved to be a safer choice because he was more circumspect on the issue. Seward had to settle for secretary of state, him and Abe stitching an administration together by handing out bribes as well as jobs.' Wilkeson paused to take wine.

'Tell you what, George. I'll fix you an invitation when he next throws money at his future. I'm acquainted with his cerebral, statuesque wife Frances, who is an abolitionist to the core and supporter of the Underground Railway, but more to the point is in charge of Seward's banqueting. That being said, I've heard recently that she is blowing cold about catering for Henry, as she calls him, and his habit of buttering up Washington society. But, I'm sure you will find such a gathering entertaining.'

Washburn returned to his room much better prepared for acquainting himself with military matters than when he had checked in at Willard's that afternoon, thanks mainly to Sam Wilkeson's willingness to impart knowledge. Before retiring, he parted the drapes and peered out over the dim gaslights of Pennsylvania Avenue toward Capitol Hill, trying to make out the site of the Congress building under construction somewhere out there.

For the rest of August Washburn busied himself observing military comings and goings, grasping the difference between ranks and regalia, corps, divisions, battalions and regiments, and listening to bugle calls, the army's birdsong. He attended end-of-the-day briefings with Wilkeson or Hill before earwigging the commentators' rumor factory. Dozens of Bohemians and correspondents paced the streets sniffing for a hint, a slip of tongue or a lucky break to give them an edge over competitors, the *Tribune's* men among them, no expense spared. Everyone felt the inertia and guessed at how long it may last.

Adams Hill had become an institution in Washington soon after he vacated the night editor's desk in New York and moved to the capital at the start of the war. The bespectacled little man's high-pitched voice was heard day and night in government corridors and Willard's public rooms. Washburn assessed the frail, near-sighted Hill to be an awkward introvert, but conceded that he possessed a nose for news, and a nose for gathering news, like no other. Hill's nightly letter to Gay contained snippets, gossip, evaluations and speculations on the army, the politicians, the administration and the state of Union. Sometimes he addressed the Rookery as many as four times in a day. He assigned correspondents, recruited new men, found mounts for them, hastened their copy, and acted as Gay's confidential adviser. He used the back room in the office for stolen interviews and copying confidential documents from the legion of sources he had cultivated in Washington. Hill listed among his confidants the president's secretary, the secretary of the treasury, top-ranking officials in the navy and war department, the speaker of the house, and more than a handful of senators and representatives. He personified the kind of journalism that Washburn came to admire and tried to practice. The rhetoric, bombast and *belles-lettres* so favored by Greeley and the old school was being supplanted by speed, efficiency and the urgency for news. This was probably the cause of Greeley's dim view of his Washington backroom boy.

'Mr Greeley's good opinion I am sorry not to possess, but Gay knows that I'm a good investment,' Hill confided to his fellow Harvard law graduate late one night in the saloon at Willard's.

Hill and Wilkeson and their multiple talents kept the *Tribune* well ahead of its New York rivals for influence and circulation, particularly the *Herald* despite its practice of flinging men and money at war coverage like none other. In particular, Hill kept his ferret's nose on Lincoln's flirtation with the emancipation issue.

'Abe's itching to add freedom for slaves to the cause of preserving the Union, but he can't proclaim until his generals win some battles,' Hill said as he was guiding Washburn through significant episodes of the discourse one evening. 'Abe has been chewing over this a long time. He was among the audience at the Smithsonian last winter when Greeley lectured on the desirability of freeing the slaves. Then Senator Sumner pressed him to introduce his decree of emancipation on fourth of July, so he must have had a draft in his pocket by that date at the very least. The argument against the decree was the fear of driving more slave states into the arms of the Confederacy. Abe was also wary of the Confiscation Act that decreed that slaves owned by persons aiding the rebellion shall be freed. He insisted on amendments before signing. That made me wonder. I think Lincoln misread the support for the bill among voters, and I told Gay so.

'So at the end of the month, July that is, Gay wrote to Lincoln quoting a typical reader's letter submitted for publication. This fella, George Rathbun was his name, accused the president of hanging back and leaving the country to drift. Abe responded by asking Gay to bring Rathbun to meet him. So ten days later, Gay's at the White House – Rathbun declined the invitation – and Abe's going round in circles. Gay presses for emancipation while Abe argues against himself, parrying with anecdotes. Gay then switches the subject and asks if the Potomac army is going to join up with Pope's, and queries if McClellan's going to be given command of the whole caboodle. Abe, not surprisingly, stonewalls. He stays silent for several minutes while rummaging in his desk, and then he mutters "I shouldn't wonder".

'All this time,' Hill continues, 'Greeley stays aloof, but is getting impatient. Eventually he orders Gay to publish his great blast addressed to the president, "The Prayer of Twenty Millions", which you'll have seen. Basically, it alleges that slavery is the cause and base of treason, and demands enforcement of the Confiscation Act. Unfortunately, it came a day sooner than Gilmore and myself found ...'

'Who's Gilmore?'

'James R Gilmore, the shadowy go-between for the Rookery and the White House. Anyway, we learned that Lincoln had prepared a proclamation three weeks beforehand, but kept it in his desk drawer because of opposition from some cabinet members. He replied to Greeley's outburst by saying,' and here Hill shuffled cuttings about until he found what he wanted, '"If there is perceptible in it an impatient and dictatorial tone, I waive it in deference to an old friend whose heart I have always supposed to be right ... What I do about slavery and the colored race, I do because I believe it helps to save the Union; and what I forbear, I forbear because I do *not* believe it would help to save the Union." The president also said,' Hill continued, 'that he believed Gay to be a truly good and wise man. So Abe clearly wanted the *Tribune* behind him. Then came Gay's reaction, saying that the president, and I quote, "has infused hope among us at the North who are anxiously awaiting that move on your part which they believe will end the rebellion by removing its cause".

After a further pause and a shuffle of papers, Hill continued: 'Wendell Phillips, whom I believe you know,' and Washburn nodded acquiescence, 'sent in some choice sentiments which I have here, awaiting the light of day. "If the proclamation of emancipation is possible at any time from Lincoln, which I somewhat doubt, it will be wrung from him only by fear. He's a spaniel by nature – nothing broad, generous or high-hearted about him".'

Over the ensuing days, Washburn joined the competition among newspaper men to glean what politicians and generals were plotting, while their proprietors locked horns to increase circulation and justify their eye-watering investments in men and machinery. He recognized Gay's pivotal role at the *Tribune*. From his sudden springtime appointment as managing editor, Gay earned a reputation for rallying reporters and editors to exertion by a mixture of encouragement, needling and silence. He injected devotion to drive the *Tribune* onwards. Wilkeson appraised the *Trib* as 'the best edited paper in America; in all respects, the most carefully, ably, and interestingly edited.' The London *Spectator* quoted Edward Dicey's comment that the *Tribune* was 'better printed, more thoughtfully written and more carefully got up than any of its contemporaries.'

The *Tribune* may have been outmanned by the *Herald*, but Gay spread his coverage dexterously over action in the peninsular while second-guessing what might occur in Maryland and the capital.

His instruction to Washburn to stay with McClellan effectively put Washburn at the head of the *Trib* scribes monitoring movements of the Army of the Potomac. Gay cabled Albert Richardson to abandon his post in Cincinnati and report to Washburn. He dispatched Joseph Rhinehart Sypher to Harrisburg and D J Kinney to Frederick, towns in locations of strategic importance. He assigned Charles A Page and John Evans, the latter a red-whiskered clerk in the treasury department recruited to the *Trib* by Hill, to observe troop movements around Washington. He ordered Nathaniel Paige to seek Washburn out when his tour on the peninsular finished.

At the end of August Washburn enjoyed a soirée at Secretary of State Seward's mansion, a pleasant diversion from heightening tension in the capital. Washington's hierarchy was gathered together to score points against one another. Washburn, remembering Wilkeson's remark that Mrs Frances Seward was in charge of guest lists and menus, made straight for her. She was easily recognizable, an apparition in braided chignon disguising a breath-constricting corset. No sooner had he introduced himself as the *Tribune* did she confide how she had grown to hate these parties, what with men's intellectual degradation of women while they paid homage to their charms.

'This is the last time I shall be hostess,' she confided to Washburn. 'Somehow such lavish fare and behavior seems out of place when Washington is almost under siege and when our president invests more importance on the preservation of the Union than the liberty of four million people. I intimated to Henry that this was not a time to feast, but he ignored my advice.'

Nevertheless, the elegant Mrs Seward had scoured the capital's markets with her daughter Fanny and laid on a banquet of oysters, turkey, ham, tongue, chicken salad, eggs and celery, not to mention turtle, terrapin, lobster, eels, frogs and treats from the bakery – all washed down by the best French wines. Fanny, who appeared at her mother's side to be directed to accompany Washburn to the buffet, wrinkled her nose when they reached the table.

'I can't eat terrapin or turtle,' she said, 'or eels and frogs.'

As August ran out, Pope's Army of Virginia confronted Lee's Army of Northern Virginia at Bull's Run, the same ground where the Rebels had faced Union forces a year previously. Washington watched anxiously as Lee triumphed again in a maneuver launched after Stonewall Jackson overran the Union supply depot at Manassas Junction. The first that Pope heard of the disaster was when the telegraph to Washington went dead on 26 August, followed by the connection between the Orange and Alexandria Railroad's junction with the army's main supply base. The last message of the Manassas telegrapher – circulated widely in Willard's – said ominously: 'No 6 train fired into at Bristoe by some say 500 cavalry …' The Rebels were astride Pope's supply line.

Armed with this news, Wilkeson attempted to confront Stanton, the secretary of war. While Washburn engaged the custodian at the portal of the war department, Wilkeson reached the telegraph room just in time to see Lincoln cross the White House grounds and enter by a side door. The president's face drained of color as he shuffled through the flimsy tissues of the morning's dispatches. He rasped an order through the open door of Stanton's boudoir that reinforcements be sent to Pope immediately, before stepping out briskly to return to the White House. Stanton flustered into the telegraph room and broke off dictating McClellan's marching orders as he caught sight of Wilkeson. 'Why is a press man loose in the war department?' he roared, and ordered an aide to show the door to the *Tribune*.

Washburn wandered the camps of Alexandria searching for signs of troops making ready to march, and he soon grasped the weight of Halleck's burden. It fell to the commander-in-chief to get McClellan moving, having personally vested the leadership of two armies in the Young Napoleon on the grounds that he was the general who fell least short of desirable talents. Melding the straggling Virginia army with the Potomac was like mixing oil with water, an exercise unaided by the derision in which many officers held Pope.

Washburn realized the strength of this feeling when he ran into Charles Francis Adams, a familiar Bostonian, and asked after his father, the present ambassador to the Court of St James's in London.

'Father's having a tough time diverting the British government's love of the South because of the lucrative cotton trade, despite outlawing the slavery that underpinned its wealthy empire,' Adams Jr told him. As Washburn ordered whiskey in the Willard's plushest saloon, Adams Jr shared his list of bombshells gleaned from staff officers at the war department and his own experiences with the First Massachusetts Cavalry, intelligence that he had just sent to Adams Sr.

'I asked my father did he know that Washington is in more danger than it has ever been? That we should be in Richmond but for the jealousy of McDowell, Pope's second-in-command? That Pope is a humbug, and known to be an outgeneraled humbug by the very people who appointed him? That small men with selfish motives control the war without any central power to put them in bounds? It's terrifying … Our rulers seem to me to be crazy. They've ripened the Union for a terrible panic while leading the army into the danger zone of utter demoralization, and they've filled the air with treachery.' He paused. 'Leastways, that's how it looks from the saddle in the First Massachusetts! Stick that in your *Tribune!*' Said with a grin.

At the Willard, Pope was portrayed as a pinch of owl dung and condemned to hanging for infamous conduct. But this was neither a possible nor politic moment in which to step him down. It was, however, the moment to send him assistance. McClellan answered Halleck's appeal by announcing that he would order his Sixth Corps to Pope's aid immediately, but he did not do so. His feeble excuse was a shortage of artillery horses, cavalry and supply wagons. Better, he argued, to make defense of the capital, now very much under threat, the first priority, was it not?

Piecing all this together, Washburn painted himself a picture of the contrasts and similarities of the commanders who held the fate of the Union in their hands. McClellan, the Young Napoleon, martial in bearing, youthful organizer, a remote figure who yet commanded presence among the lower ranks. Halleck 'Old Brains', dumpy and paunchy, swim-eyed deskman without presence. Both versed in bureaucratic survival: cautious, deflectors of responsibility, protectors of flanks and rear from hostile fire of critics. The mutual practice of their art began with McClellan's message from his Potomac HQ in Alexandria.

It was no wonder that Washington's streets filled with anxiety when fueled by muffled thunder of supply trains and galloping urgency of mud-spattered orderlies. After the Rebels checkmated the Union battalions in the peninsular, pallid, bloodied soldiers stalked the capital with tales of their regiment's annihilation, and long lines of avalanches delivered bruised and battered victims to sanctuary. All the talk on doorsteps was of treachery and malfeasance. One evening, Washburn came across a group of agitated journalists exchanging anecdotes outside the telegraph office. 'The war department has barred us from using the telegraph,' the man from the *Chicago Times* complained.

The New York *Tribune* stirred matters in an impetuous piece stating that Major General Nathaniel Banks's corps of Pope's army had been cut to pieces, and it was rumored that the president had relieved McClellan of his command and denounced him as a traitor. A fuming White House issued a swift denial, and the edition was suppressed. Wilkeson was embarrassed. He had sent notice of the rumor to the Rookery, neither endorsing nor intending it for publication unless and until it could be verified.

'In his dark, frustrated moments, Abe would surely like to denounce Mac, who's no friend of the abolition cause and leads Abe a merry gavotte, but I'll wager my dancing shoes that he hasn't acted so,' Wilkeson opined to Washburn. 'Abe needs action in the field, while Mac courts popularity with his men with supplies of victuals and ordnance, for which you cannot fault him. Maybe it *is* votes he's after, for he certainly has presidential ambitions.'

The two *Tribune* men shared concern that inflammatory items of this sort did not help their paper's desire, as the news sheet with the highest circulation among Federal troops, to get close to McClellan.

Next day, Lincoln faced down the rumor by placing fortifications and forces for the defense of the capital under McClellan's command on the grounds that the general will man the defenses swiftly and lick demoralized troops into shape. Several members of Lincoln's cabinet demurred, but the president avowed his commander-in-chief's assurance, at least in public, that McClellan was the best general for the job.

6

Scout's Honor

Wednesday, 10 September 1862, Frederick, Maryland

Come the afternoon of 4 September an electric charge hit the telegraph room at the war department. The lookout station on Sugar Loaf Mountain reported that Lee's army was fording the Potomac and heading into Maryland. Lieutenant Brinkerhoff Miner's dispatch said that a train of seventy-five wagons was observed on the move from Leesburg toward Edwards Ferry, and that continuous clouds of dust were seen on roads leading to a large wagon park near the turnpike about five miles southeast of Leesburg. It concluded: 'The enemy are now shelling the aqueduct over Monocacy river, and I judge are attempting to cross, from reports of musketry heard.'

Despite the war department's reluctance to give credence to the report, word flew through the capital when a farmer on his lathered horse careened down Pennsylvania Avenue shouting the news. Editors pored over maps, and on the night of the fifth, McClellan's Six Corps, comprising 84,000 men, began trundling out of Washington. Their destination was Frederick, a town close to the Monocacy aqueduct on the Hagerstown road to the northwest of the capital, where McClellan evidently believed Lee to be bound.

George Washburn rode along, elated at the Federal army's heave into action. With his equipment gathered about him, he called at the *Tribune* office on his way out of town to pick up any last orders from Gay or news of Paige and Richardson, with whom he must liaise in the action ahead. There was nothing from the Rookery or from the correspondents, but one letter awaited him. He tried to look nonchalant as he tore at the envelope to glance at its content. Outside, with the note in his breast pocket, he could no longer control the frisson of excitement as he cantered down the street in search of the Young Napoleon.

'Mr Washburn,' it began, 'you are the tease of the Bohemians, I do declare, and flattery may well reward the handsomest man to make the descent into Pfaff's cave for many a month. The discreet Herr Charlie knows where to find me when I am in the city, so you should write him when in New York if you want to see your angel with aura.'

On 10 September, 100,000 of McClellan's men were camped in a twenty-five-mile arc from the Potomac to the northwest, poised to confront Lee at Frederick. Washburn stayed at a safe distance from the high command. Being neither an official correspondent nor an official aide, he relied on his navy brass-buttoned coat and slouch hat to pass for officer garb in the vicinity of the farmhouse that served as McClellan's HQ. He tethered his horse at the stable under the charge of a boy glad of extra dollars, and passed the time of day with aides as they came and went. This gave him entrée to the officers' mess. If asked his pedigree, he intimated the half-truth that he was on General Sedgwick's staff, confident that the said general was not in the vicinity. The truth was that he had crossed paths with Sedgwick in the lobby at Willard's and, knowing him to be sympathetic to the press, remarked that he was looking for an opportunity to go with the troops. Sedgwick said simply, 'Then come along with me.'

Thus the Bohemian assumed the role of aide-de-camp without responsibility, able to observe McClellan up to his elbows in what he was good at. For hour after hour the commander deployed infantry, cavalry, artillery and supply trains to service them, while ably demonstrating his talent for prevarication in the face of the enemy. The tension between McClellan and his commander-in-chief, 'Old Brains' Halleck, was plain to see. Neither Halleck nor Lincoln could gainsay McClellan's frequent demands for more troops on the grounds that he was outnumbered.

Washburn's break came at the foot of the lane leading to the army's farmstead headquarters, where a sutler had parked his wagon beside the Frederick road. A crowd of officers was purchasing supplementary rations of canned meats and pastries, tobacco and toiletries. While surveying the goods on offer, which to his surprise included books, Washburn overheard the man in front ask quietly for a newspaper. The sutler winked and produced a *Tribune* from the dark recess of his cart. When Washburn made the same request, the sutler pretended not to hear until Washburn's proffered handful of copperheads changed his mind.

The officer already had his nose in his *Tribune* when Washburn caught up with him to wonder out loud what revelations were to be found in the day's news. They fell into conversation as they set off up the track with their purchases. The officer introduced himself as Lieutenant-Colonel David H Strother, aide to General McClellan, and was soon quoting Wilkeson's days-old speculation on Lee's tactics, and how McClellan should respond. Then, pulling a previous edition of the *Tribune* out of his haversack, he pointed to a poignant piece on the state of the Union and its generals as he passed it to Washburn.

The passage was datelined 8 September and said:

The enemy has no more men, not so much ordnance, nor provisions, nor transportation facilities, nor nearly so much encumbering baggage but he has outgeneraled us from Slaughter Mountain to Edward's Ferry, and God knows but he will do so hereafter. Make your display of capital headings to your war news, harp upon our driving the enemy a mile this morning, and four rods the day after tomorrow, but take your map and see how that enemy has crowded us miles upon miles, and leagues upon leagues, from Culpepper to the very gates of the Capital ... this is the plain, unvarnished truth; we have been whipped by an inferior force of inferior men, better handled than our own.

Washburn gulped, and then confided his real identity. Strother didn't blink, and to Washburn's relief seemed pleased to have found an ear for his concerns. 'I should be careful what I say,' said the officer. 'The army has forbidden us to talk to newsmen, but I don't hold with that. Silence will only stir rumor, not scotch it. I agree with the sentiments expressed here,' and he stuffed the paper back into the haversack.

Trees of heaven shaded the bendy farm track, and gaps in the foliage looked out over fields as far as the eye could see. With the exception of acres yet to be harvested, tipi-like conical tents, designed by Major Sibley to replace the army's old French-style bell tents, covered every un-plowed hectare with canvas. Each tent was home to twenty infantrymen who marched, messed and fought together. Smoke rose from improvised field kitchens and seeped from the canvas vents of tents, and the mouth-watering smell of roasting meat prevailed over the vile odor emitted by leaves of heaven trees if you should be unlucky enough, as Washburn was, to crush one underfoot.

'My God, that's disgusting. Smells like cat's urine.'

'Well, we're fortunate not to be here in June, the worst month of the year to be near a heaven tree,' Strother said. 'They can stun an ox in June, their perfume's so strong.'

Snatches of popular songs and trills of dancing fiddles, strumming banjos and wailing harmonicas wafted upwards on the afternoon air.

'The mood will be different when they are faced with besieging Frederick,' Strother said, sensing Washburn's unspoken thought.

'So have you any idea what McClellan's going to do?' Washburn asked.

'Frankly, the Young Napoleon doesn't know whether he's coming or going,' Strother said, almost spitting the officers' nickname for their commander. 'And I should know because my job is to dispatch Napoleon's orders and make sure that every commander entitled to a copy receives one. He doesn't know where Lee is or where Lee is intent on going. I took down a message two or so days ago in which he told Halleck that he was not yet satisfied that Lee had crossed the Potomac in any large force, despite the intelligence sent from the post on Sugar Loaf Mountain. He said that as soon as he finds out where to strike he'll be after them without an hour's delay.'

Strother paused before continuing

'Only an hour's delay? A miracle for sure! You can't start this army up in a day! Twenty-four hours is about as speedy as McClellan can manage.'

Strother was equally scornful of the intelligence gathered by the cavalry under General Alfred Pleasonton, who had been sent ahead to locate the enemy and his intentions. 'Pleasonton was hampered by superior Rebel cavalry and forced to rely on relayed mixed messages and unreliable second-hand sources. An Irishman wandering in the countryside told him that the

Rebel target was Baltimore. Pleasonton passed to McClellan that Lee and Jackson, though apparently bound for Frederick, were aiming for Washington, a message perhaps calculated to ignite McClellan's innately elaborate sense of caution. Canny officers suspected a plant by a Confederate agent when they heard a sudden convergence of reports naming Baltimore as the objective.'

The most plausible and accurate intelligence, Strother continued, was contained in a telegram from a supervisor on the Baltimore and Ohio Railroad whose attempt to run a locomotive to Harper's Ferry was thwarted by a large Rebel force some miles short of Frederick. He added that there was a massive munitions store at the ferry where the Potomac and Shenandoah rivers converge, with only a small Union garrison to defend it.

'It's an obvious target for Lee, but the railroad man's message went unheeded by cocksure Pleasonton. And nothing more has been heard from Lieutenant Miner, who first raised the alarm from the Sugar Loaf. That suggests that he's fallen to the enemy or is trapped behind the lines.'

As Strother revealed more and more contrary figures, Washburn recognized the survival trait that he had attributed to McClellan and Halleck. Napoleon McClellan was listening only to figures he wished to hear, protecting his rear while Little Mac McClellan courted favor among the ranks, refusing to budge until everything was to his and his men's satisfaction. For his part, Halleck was probably fudging figures to keep the president off his back.

'What Pleasonton has probably got right is that the whole of Lee's invading army has crossed the Potomac,' Strother said. 'But estimates of its size range wildly. The consensus among the staff officers is thirty thousand, but there was an unsubstantiated story floating about that forty thousand reinforcements were on their way from Tennessee. When McClellan reached Rockville, twelve miles off Frederick, he informed Washington that he would be "after the enemy within the hour". That evening, Pleasonton reported that a hundred thousand Rebels had crossed the river.'

He waived his arms in a futile gesture.

'How they glean such garbage I don't know. Pleasonton said he learned it from Rebel officers and citizens along the route. Mac reported the figures to Halleck without embellishment, but by implication he's asking for reinforcements, which is his old refrain. He's now convinced we're outnumbered three to one. He won't listen to anyone who doubts him. Next day, on the ninth, he reported to Halleck that Pleasonton's source was an unreliable guerrilla, name of Captain White. There was no longer any doubt that the enemy was in and about Frederick, nor that the garrison at the ferry would fall to Lee. As dusk fell, McClellan the magician endorsed Captain White's alleged assertion by telegraphing Halleck that Jackson and Longstreet have a hundred and ten thousand men near Frederick, while assuring the chief that he was in a position to watch them closely. If you ask me, all he *will* do is watch them closely.'

It was now obvious to Washburn, casting through his notes on every estimate of Rebel strength noted, that the true total was nowhere near the figure in McClellan's head. Besides, Lee's army was known to be losing stragglers and deserters by the hour.

'I share the skepticism that my Washington colleague Wilkeson puts on Rebel estimates,' Washburn said. 'He reckons that such figures are likely enhanced by civilians along the way who either hold out a hand of friendship to Lee's and Jackson's men, or rejoice in their departure. Either way they exaggerate, and men like Jackson know it, and know how to braggart it to good effect.'

On the morning of the tenth, McClellan ordered further advance toward Frederick. Strother told Washburn that when the president gently probed for news of action, the general's response was that his scouts and spies were pushed forward in every direction. What he didn't say, Strother said, was that the cavalry reported the enemy to be moving out of Frederick.

'Who would you say we are watching here, Little Mac or Young Napoleon?'

Strother scoffed. 'The real Napoleon was half McClellan's age and twice the soldier when he conquered Europe. I prefer the men's sobriquet. Somehow he excites their confidence. He doesn't expect too much, doesn't drive them with forced marches like Jackson does.'

The pair had long reached the top of the hill where the requisitioned farmhouse that served as HQ enjoyed good views over the valley and the mountain. Strother was hailed by a man sitting at an easel beside a wagon whom he introduced to Washburn as 'McClellan's favored artist, Mr Winslow Homer of *Harper's Weekly*.'

Homer scoffed. 'Only when Abe wants a daub of victory.'

'Doesn't he fear that pictures from the war in *Harper's* might be of value to the Rebels?' Washburn asked.

'No, he thinks my work is as likely to confuse them.'

When Homer was out of hearing, Strother remarked that exaggerated pictures of the illustrated weeklies provoked much merriment among the officers. 'The *Cincinnati Gazette* suggested that those who draw their conceptions of the appearance of Rebel soldiery from *Harper's* would hardly recognize one on sight. *Harper's* and *Frank Leslie's* and the *Illustrated News* have all accused one another of drawing battle scenes in the office. The staff officers refer to Homer's paper as *Harper's Weakly*, spelled with an "a", if you follow me.'

Washburn turned the conversation to another tack. 'What do you know of Pinkerton? I heard in Washington that McClellan is using his detective agency for espionage and interrogation of prisoners.'

'Sure, that bivouac yonder belongs to Pinkertons,' Strother said, pointing toward a paddock by the stables. 'There's a fella amongst them, his name will come to me, who draws great maps, much more useful to us than Homer and his imaginative friends, entertaining as they may be. But whatever the Pinkertons produce, there's no sign from where I sit that McClellan takes any notice. My guess is that Pinkerton has been thrust upon him, so he's indulging him while ignoring his advice.'

Later, wandering with intent near the detectives' tent, Washburn was pulled up short by the sight of a tall figure tending a steed in the paddock. The man looked familiar, but the reporter couldn't place him. A censor from Pope's retinue, a rider from Frémont's? A student from Harvard or a legal beagle in a Boston courtroom? He strolled over to the paddock and introduced himself with 'Fine horse you have there, sir, if I may say so!'

'You may indeed, sir. I'm fortunate to have found Gimlet, the demand for horses being what it is.' He looked the horse in the eye and stroked its nose with affection.

'Are you with the detective agency? I guess a good horse is essential in your kind of work, just as in mine.'

'And what might that be?' inquired he who was yet to offer a clue of his identity. 'Let me guess. You are a vitalizer? A paymaster? Not a general, surely? Or a Confed scoundrel?' Said with a wry smile.

'I'm George Washburn, aide-de-camp to General Sedgwick and indulged by him as correspondent of the New York *Tribune*, at your service.'

'Aha, then I shall have to stay my tongue. My task is to draw field maps of my scouting exploits for our commander.'

'I can't help thinking that we've met before,' Washburn said, 'but I can't place you. I'm sure I haven't crossed paths with many cartographers, if any.'

'You must meet all sorts in your line of business. I must say that your sheet is better informed than most. Better than the army, quite often. I wonder, between you and me, Mr Washburn, why we Pinkertons bother to interrogate deserters and prisoners or scout the territory, for all the notice McClellan takes of our intelligence. He compliments me on my skills as a map maker, and then ignores what my maps are saying to him.'

'That's what my colleague in Washington says, mister, err, what did you say your name was? He thinks that McClellan is obsessed with exaggerating the enemy's head count to justify demanding reinforcements at every turn, to the fury of General Halleck, the commander-in-chief.'

'I don't believe I did, sir, but since you inquire, it's Babcock, John C Babcock, formerly of the Chicago Sturges Rifles, and a practicing architect in that city. My talents at maps and topographical depiction, latterly Confederate battle movements more than anything else, came to the attention of Mr Pinkerton and General McClellan, and so I now find myself to be the principal scout for the Army of the Potomac. At your service! And I would wager that your man in Washington is not far off the mark. Of course, the nature of surveying means that Pinkertons are not always dead accurate. And,' glancing about conspiratorially, 'there is also

Mr Pinkerton's interest in continuing to produce information for which the army is grateful. Putting food on the table and all that. But there's many a snare twixt scouting intelligence and McClellan's reports to General Halleck, I troth.'

That was it. Washburn had met Babcock in Boston when the architect from Chicago turned up at the shed and asked to borrow a skiff in which to explore the Charles River.

'Are you an oarsman, Mr Babcock? Did you call at the Union Boat Club in Boston a couple of years back? I was secretary there and I seem to remember ...'

'... bringing compliments from the Metropolitan Rowing Club of Chicago, yes! Let me see, you once rowed for, was it, Harvard? No, Yale?'

With that, Babcock gestured toward the Pinkerton tent, and the pair were soon drinking coffee while the cartographer flipped through his sketch book of Rebel fortifications, topography, ferry crossings and doodles.

'I've something here that may interest you,' he said, turning to a depiction of an oblong piece of wood with flanges affixed to the long sides. 'I've long thought how inefficient the rowing movement is sitting on a fixed piece of wood, to say nothing of painful blisters on your backside. If we could find a way of bringing all the strength of the legs into play, we'd get a much longer stroke than is possible under the present arrangement. We could enable a man's reach to exceed his grasp, which is a line I read in a poem by a British poet, Bridges I think it was. My idea is to mount the seat on rails or runners so that you can bend your knees and bring your leg muscles into play to draw a longer arc with the oars. Even better would be to make your outriggers and foot stretcher slide while keeping your seat fixed, but I'm defeated as to how to make such a contraption work without encountering friction. Wood's too bendy, has too much give in it. I've been playing around with these ideas in Chicago, but I've a way to go before the world wakes up to such a device. This darned war is no help, either.'

'I see the logic of it,' Washburn said. 'If you ever get to make a slider, I'd like to be the first to try it out.'

During the next hour the two oarsmen were transported to the waters of Lake Michigan and the Charles River, comparing their races and jaunts, and when Washburn bade Babcock good night he had added another useful informant to his small circle of confidants.

7

The Order of Fate

Saturday, 13 September 1862, a field near Frederick
The morning after George Washburn became acquainted with the
Pinkertons, intelligence suggested that Lee's army was clearing
out of Frederick, to the tune, it was said, of *The Girl I Left Behind
Me*. McClellan ordered that camp be struck at dawn on the
twelfth, and the next hours were occupied speculating on where
Lee was going. Washburn loitered in the hope that someone
would commandeer him for an errand, and Strother told him of
an allegation by a citizen that Lee found his hostile reception in
Frederick disappointing. If true, this was ammunition for those
critics of McClellan who thought Lee would head back to the
Potomac and shelter in the Shenandoah Valley.

'McClellan's reply to Lincoln's telegraph demanding news was
to say that if Harper's Ferry is still in our hands, it can be defended,
but that if the Rebels are marching toward Pennsylvania, as some
speculate, he shall soon be up with them,' Strother said, taking in
breath before muttering angrily: 'I disagree with both suppositions.
Harper's is as defendable as a cat in hell, and Lee's not about to
go to see the sights in Baltimore or Philly. Fighting Joe Hooker
says although Lee's men appear headed up the Hagerstown road
toward Harrisburg, he's satisfied they have no more intention of
going to Pennsylvania than they have of going to heaven. Always
heed Fighting Joe.

'When it comes to the ferry,' he continued, 'there's a pitiful
garrison there to protect our vast armory, and Lee's sure to get

between us and it. Unless we stop him fording the Potomac, he'll skedaddle back to the Shenandoah with half of the Union's munitions. Have you seen Harper's Ferry? It's a landscape of hell where the Potomac meets the Shenandoah and Maryland meets West Virginia, a place wrecked by successive armies having their way. There are steep bluffs on every hand looking over the charred ruins of a once pretty settlement, where houses and hotels, arsenals and stores, railroads and workshops now mingle in a blackened mash of Hades. It's futile for the garrison to hold out unless it has control of the heights, which it hasn't. The evidence is all in the Pinkerton scout's map which I conveyed to the general a couple of days ago.'

Babcock's work, Washburn surmised. Reaching in excess of his grasp.

At first light on September's glorious twelfth, column after column of the Army of the Potomac swung out through corn meadows and green hills toward Frederick, led by Colonel Augustus Moor's cavalry, soon to be engaging the Rebel rear guard among the clustered spires around the town's main street. Carbines cracked, troopers were unseated, and a cannon rent men and horses before it was upended into a ditch. The day was still young when Federal infantrymen entered one end of the town as the rump of Lee's troops trotted out of the other. Citizens emerged gingerly to show their pleasure at being in the Union again.

At ten o'clock Strother had sent McClellan's message to the White House via the restored telegraph link at the Baltimore and Ohio Railroad's depot: 'Rebels headed for Hagerstown and Harper's Ferry.'

While his aides requisitioned a farm for his new HQ, McClellan trotted bareheaded through the town at the head of his guard, acknowledging salutations from the citizenry at every turn. Elderly ladies wept buckets and young ladies tossed bouquets from balconies. Union flags brightened the streets, and hands were extended from all sides.

Washburn followed his progress, marveling at the commander's ability to about face from Young Napoleon to Little Mac, from remote commander to savior with the common touch. By late afternoon the reporter had filled several pages with townsfolk conversation, including the story of fourscore-years-and-ten Barbara Freitchie engaging Stonewall Jackson's nobler nature when his troops tried to shoot down her Union flag. 'Whoever touches a hair of yon gray head dies like a dog,' hollers Stonewall. 'March on!' And Barbara flew her flag defiantly through the Rebel occupation. Back at the farm, Washburn found a shady spot and wrote a description of the relief of Frederick to send to the *Tribune*. He decided to risk sending it through the military censor, whom he figured would be hard pressed to object to some rare good news.

Noon next day brought a sudden stir at field HQ. An aide summarily shooed a citizens' delegation from the porch, blurting that General McClellan was engaged in pressing army business. Simultaneously, Strother appeared in the yard and pointed a dispatch rider toward the town. Turning on his heel, he beckoned Washburn over as the courier clattered off at a gallop.

'Mac's sent an extraordinary message to Lincoln,' he said. 'He says he has all the plans of the Rebels and that no time will be lost. Somebody in the Twenty-Seventh Indiana apparently found Lee's order to his generals in the field where they set up their bivouac. I've never seen such a positive message from Mac. Previously he's only sent a stream of preposterous reasons for delay.'

'Have you seen the order?' asks Washburn.

'Only glanced over it. McClellan's waving it about like he's struck gold. A corporal found it in long grass still warm from the hand that dropped it. There were three cigars wrapped in it, so they say. Addressed to all the commanders and signed by Lee's adjutant. As luck has it, one of our aides recognized the adjutant's name from West Point before the war, and so confirms that it's genuine.'

'So we know where we're going?'

'You won't be surprised to hear that Lee is hell bent on Harper's Ferry, with Jackson and Longstreet directed to close there. McClellan's sent Pleasonton's cavalry to shadow them and is intent on plugging the gaps through South Mountain. Like I said before, defending the armory at the ferry's a hopeless quest, but we should be able to tan Lee's hide nevertheless.'

Just then, a youth sprawled under a huge black walnut tree waved to Washburn, scrambled to his feet and introduced himself as Nathaniel Paige.

'Glad to catch you,' Washburn said. 'Do I call you Nat or Nathaniel? Have you come directly from the peninsular?'

The two *Tribune* men quickly exchanged credentials, and Washburn shared what he had just gleaned.

'Well,' said Paige, 'you'll never wager a guess what I have, between you and me. Call me Nat, by the way. Colonel Key, the judge advocate at headquarters, told me in confidence that a group of disaffected Yankee officers would like to countermarch on Washington and force the old women of the administration – that's how he put it – to sue for peace and end the fight without interfering with slavery. "They are fighting for a boundary line, not for a Union," is how Key whispered it to me. "I'm going to put a stop to such talk. McClellan is not a party to it," he said. I don't know how serious is the plot, but you know as well as I that McClellan's sympathies lie not with old Abe. I hear that McClellan writes often to that wife of his. I'd sure love to read what he says to her ...'

'Sounds like Fitz, what was his name, Fitz Henry Warren, still making mischief out there,' Washburn muttered, half to himself.

He asked Paige what he knew about the supposed scandal of the peninsular female spy.

'You mean Belle? Belle Boyd the Rebel temptress, the Confederate spy, the accomplished prostitute who the *Herald* calls the Siren of Shenandoah? Good line, that last one. Belle was certainly a sensation. She is an enigma. She's no beauty, but she's viscerally attractive. I had the good fortune to be granted an interview, and she owned up to spying – knows the name of every officer in the Rebel army – but took fierce offense at attacks on her virtue. She has a superb figure, tall, statuesque, intelligent face, black eyes set in sharp features, and she's a tasteful dresser. She's barely into her twenties. She certainly doesn't give off the aura of a lady of the night, and she's no saloon bar whore ...'

'She didn't make advances on you, then?'

'Far from it, though her attire is challenging. She wears a Rebel soldier's belt round her waist, sometimes with a revolver tucked into it, and a velvet band bearing the seven stars of the Confederacy across her forehead. She wears a golden necklace depicting a palmetto tree under her elegant chin. And I'm told she can behave with utter abandon and bearing, in pert manner slaying every lieutenant and captain who sets eyes on her. Attracted by wantonness. One wonders why such a flirt was allowed to go at will into Federal camps.'

He looked wide-eyed at Washburn and continued:

'What I didn't write except in a note to Gay was that she spent four hours closeted alone with General Shields, but when I put the question to him later, the general said he didn't think she was what the camp gossip assumed her to be. Well, he wouldn't think it out loud, would he? Was his offer rejected? He's either naive or a liar. She was caught hiding in a cupboard with the intention of passing Shields's orders to Stonewall Jackson. But then, her dash eventually led to the unveiling of a lively source. She was jailed in Old Capitol Prison, but I heard that she has already been released.'

Washburn and Paige squatted under their walnut tree and scrutinized Washburn's map to seek out McClellan's options. South Mountain was a barrier on the road to Hagerstown, some ten miles onwards from Frederick. If the Army of the Potomac could plug the gaps that bisect the range, Lee's men would have to march southwest toward crossing points on the Potomac to reach the sanctuary of Virginia and the Shenandoah. If McClellan has superior numbers, which the *Tribune* men knew to be the case, he could seal any threat to Washington or Pennsylvania and chase Lee into the Potomac at the same time. It was a moot point whether the Feds would be able to save their garrison at Harper's Ferry, pinned down as it was by Rebel divisions on the three heights brooding over the confluence of the rivers below. But there was no reason, Washburn asserted, why McClellan shouldn't pursue Lee into Virginia. Unless the general was to kill time once more by alleging that he must await reinforcements.

'I guess one way or the other,' Washburn said, pulling himself up, 'we might get to see a Union advance and a Rebel retreat. That would put us in the van of the Bohemian Brigade.'

He shared his informant's bet with Paige that McClellan was

heading the whole of his army to South Mountain.

'I'll stick with Mac and Hooker, whose corps is leading. You go with Franklin. That way we'll cover both Turner's and Crampton's gaps. Have you seen Richardson? Gay's latest note said he's headed our way.'

Paige shook his head while Washburn stabbed South Mountain on his map before folding it away. 'Let's try and meet wherever HQ happens to be in twenty-four hours to reappraise. If you should see Richardson, pass it on.'

8

Young Napoleon's Triumph

Sunday, 14 September 1862, Turner's Gap

Washburn spent a restless night. He awoke at first light tethered to his steed's bridle under his chosen black walnut tree, ready to mount and trot off as soon as a uniform stirred. He couldn't understand why no orders had been issued to move on Lee while McClellan was clutching his enemy's battle orders in his own hand, convinced that they were not a hoax. McClellan had squandered at least four hours of yesterday's daylight by failing to strike for South Mountain, in effect presenting Lee with eighteen extra hours to assemble his forces. McClellan allowed grass to grow under his feet despite the advantage proffered by the luck of a corporal. You have to wonder, Washburn wrote in his notebook before he retired that night.

As he dreamed about coffee and breakfasting on porridge followed by a hoppel poppel hash of egg, meat, potato and vegetables and his mother's apple pie, he whispered Baker's doggerel of the day to himself:

Suppose for a moment, George, my friend –
Just for a moment, you condescend
To use the means that is in your hands,
The eager muskets, the guns, and brands;
Take one bold step on the Southern sod,
And leave the issue to watchful God!
For now the Nation raises its gorge,
Waiting and watching you, tardy George!

But now, before Washburn had gotten around to unfolding his map, tardy George's tardy regiments were streaming toward South Mountain in pursuit of the Rebel army. He was soon on the move, encountering heavily wooded slopes where ravines and hollows bisected tangled undergrowth. The marching men exuded cocky confidence, but their mood would soon change if their advance met resistance where the National Road crossed the range at Turner's Gap before heading west to Boonsboro. It surely had occurred to Lee that a scatter of artillery pieces above the tree line could easily achieve the defense of level farmland high under the crest of a mountain.

The Federal troops approached the mountain in buoyant mood. Pleasonton's cavalry were in the van, followed by an infantry brigade charged with clearing the way through the gap. Washburn was mystified that Fighting Joe Hooker's First Corps, camped some dozen miles from Frederick and requiring several hours to reach Turner's, was named as first in marching order. No way would First Corps make a surprise breakthrough that morning.

Washburn attached himself to the Ohio volunteers of the Ninth Corps, known as the Kanawha Division, who were first to reach the mountain. They were met by screaming shells from a Rebel battery on the ridge. By skirting round the old road toward the village of Sharpsburg, the Kanawhas broke into open pasture, faced at the far end by a Rebel battle line entrenched behind a stone wall.

As Strother had intimated to Washburn in their brief encounter at dawn, resistance on South Mountain was not part of Lee's plan as understood by McClellan. Assuming that Lee was unaware of the fate of his 'Lost' Order 191, McClellan expected him to make haste to Harper's Ferry. But as the great Federal snake ascended the mountain, Confederate batteries lay in wait. McClellan had handed Lee a golden opportunity to halt the tardy Army of the Potomac in its tracks. As the guns breathed fire, the reporter took cover. He noted that the Union commander had brought a battle onto his head that would not be taking place if he had moved his army a day earlier.

From his position in the woods Washburn watched the Kanawhas, confident that they outnumbered the Rebels, push hard along the enemy line. A Federal crew manhandled artillery pieces close enough to fire canister until Rebel sharpshooters methodically picked off the gunners. The Feds fixed bayonets and charged behind their colors. The Rebel middle withdrew in confusion, but its flanks stood their ground and engaged in a mêlée of slashing bayonets and clubbing rifles.

The Kanawhas pressed on toward Fox's Gap and reached a homestead on the old road a mile or so from Turner's. Washburn watched warily as Rebel artillery plowed furrows in the ground at their opponents' feet. He noted that casualties were high, ammunition low and men short of wind after their hard climb. Shadows indicated that the hour was close to noon when the order came to fall back from the exposed position. There was yet no sign of Hooker's First Corps, and Rebel reinforcements at Fox's Gap neutralized any advantage gained by the Kanawhas.

Two hours later, units of Ninth Corps reached Fox's Gap, and severe fighting broke out in surrounding cornfields and pastures. A full five hours after battle commenced, Washburn noted. He was grateful for the effort he had put into recognizing regimental colors, of which there was infinite variety. He knew that identification of fighting units was important to *Tribune* readers keeping track of their neighbors' heroic deeds. He witnessed the Seventeenth Michigan and the Forty-fifth Pennsylvanian using a rail fence for cover while they faced Rebels shielded behind a stone wall. A wounded man to whom he gave water told him that the Michigan men donned dress uniform in honor of their first battle, having been under arms for scarcely two weeks. The Pennsylvanians had not seen action until this moment either. Exposed to bullets and the flaming ordnance called 'lampposts', their charge and rout of Rebels came at heavy cost.

Half the day gone, much of it up in smoke, and the Feds were yet to reach Turner's Gap. After resting his horse, Washburn re-mounted and retraced his steps down the Sharpsburg Road, putting distance between himself and the cloying odors of burning explosives, shattered hopes and spent lives. He could see the endless Federal snake writhing toward the eastern ridge across the valley, quilled with the silver slant of shouldered muskets, hearts beating in time with their drummer boys as they followed their colors.

Where the Sharpsburg Road met the National Road beneath the mountain, Washburn turned off and climbed a knoll from where he had a panoramic view of Hooker's First Corps tramping along below. It was here as he jotted down *aides de memoir* that McClellan appeared beside him astride Daniel Webster, a mounted apparition of inaction witnessing action. The First Corps singing contrasted with reverberations from the far side of the valley, the scything sound of skirmishing under billows of burning foliage; rifle fire, bugle calls and cries of casualties. The marchers who tossed their caps on sight of their hero knew nothing of his plans nor the opportunities squandered. What confronted them was the enemy of their country and flag that they loved, and they employed the time-honored emotions of patriots to wipe away the stain of defeat.

It was around four o'clock in the afternoon when the general and the correspondent exchanged words on the knoll, almost seven hours after battle commenced. Now that Hooker's men had arrived, the Federal forces were at last ready to make a coordinated attack on the Rebel flanks at Turner's Gap. By now, Washburn noted, Rebel reinforcements had dug in. 'Critical moment militarily but Mac showing air of detachment as if watching maneuver like disinterested spectator.'

When Washburn resumed his ride, he followed Hooker's ascent of the mountain, now and then adding notes for elaboration later. The First Corps launched a relentless coordinated attack on a skirmish line manned by eagle-eyed Alabamians. Hard fighting continued for several hours, during which he saw the color bearer of the Seventy-Sixth New York shot in the head after planting his flag and invoking his comrades to give the enemy hell. He was 'mustered out of the army militant and mustered into the army triumphant' in Washburn's note. Confusion reigned when the Forty-Sixth New York used up its cartridges and fell back from the firing line in the gloaming to allow the Ninth New Hampshire to replace them. The Hampshires were untrained debutantes on the battlefield, and when Rebels unleashed a volley from the woods, they nervously returned fire before the New Yorkers were out of harm's way. 'Hamps' aim too bad to hit NY troops, who threw themselves to the ground; injury avoided,' Washburn noted.

Formation was rendered impossible by Rebel artillery's tactic of raking fields to raise dust and plot furrows. But when two regiments of Rebels tried to storm a Federal battery, they stumbled into three regiments of the Eighty-Ninth New York, who were lying out of sight to defend the Union guns.

Washburn took down quotes from a group of resting infantrymen. 'The Confeds stood before us not twenty feet away but helpless with empty muskets, so we rose up and shot them down,' said one. Another wished he were back home after seeing the slaughter on the battlefield. 'Beards of the dead clotted thick with blood, and the groaning and cursing of the wounded, Federal and Confederate alike.'

While First and Ninth Corps covered flanks, a brigade headed straight up the National Road to assault the gap head on. Washburn recognized them as the Black Hat Brigade from Indiana and Wisconsin. Their commander, John Gibbon, awarded them black felt hats after they had slugged it out with Stonewall Jackson's men at Bull Run. Babcock had mentioned Gibbon to Washburn, a veteran artillerist from the old army who had a way with volunteers, promising reward for effective training and good performance. He was in the habit of allowing time off for picking black berries and other diverse pursuits.

The sun was dipping behind the mountain when the Black Hats were ordered forward, led by skirmishers and supported by two pieces of artillery. McClellan and his high command watched on a safe hillside when Federal guns scored a direct hit on a dwelling, setting fire to the roof and filling the air with animal screeches and civilian screams. The Black Hats reached the Rebel line but couldn't break through it.

It was now too murky to drive on through Turner's Gap. Washburn had enough material for a *Tribune* piece on McClellan's cautious advance toward confrontation, not forgetting the general's exclusive utterance that 'we might bite his tail'. He turned about and rode off the mountain, intent on the cook wagon at the bivouac, hoping to find Paige and Richardson before composing a dispatch from the front line. Every now and then he paused to scan the ridges guarding the gap, sniffing the persistent whiff of cordite. When darkness set in, a thousand fireflies and lightning flashes of artillery lit up the mountain. The firing finally flickered out along the summit, leaving the cries and groans of the wounded to wail faintly from the silence.

On the road back to McClellan's HQ, Washburn overhauled a stream of ambulances going his way and passed dashing dispatch riders and lumbering wagon trains heading for the mountain.

Later, fed and watered, he found Paige in the company of Albert Richardson squatting in the glow of an oil lamp in the farmyard. Richardson had just rode in, saddle sore after his non-stop journey from Wisconsin.

'Compliments of Mr Gay,' said the newcomer, 'I'm to report to you,' shaking Washburn by the hand while maintaining his prone position.

'Glad you could make it. I was beginning to worry that you wouldn't.'

'Glad to be here instead of kicking my heels in the dusty west. Not much happening there, and I soon feel itchy if I have nothing to write. Gay's instruction came just at the right time.'

Washburn trod carefully, knowing that Richardson was more experienced than he, and had been sent to McClellan's army because he was a proven scribe. He wondered why Gay hadn't appointed Richardson as field editor. Was there a flaw in his character? Was star quality lacking? Perhaps Gay knew something that Washburn didn't.

'Did you have any trouble with the army?'

'No. After Halleck's ban I spent two weeks of summer tailing other reporters, unable to attend battles legally, but then I secured an outdated pass signed by Burnside, and no picket has ever checked it, including those on my sixty-five-mile ride to get here. But I have been experienced in subterfuge ever since disguising my presence in New Orleans last year by filing to the *Tribune* in the form of letters to banks. Anyhow, the first thing I did when I arrived here was to take tea with General Marcy, on McClellan's staff. I didn't disguise what I was up to and he was curious about how I came to be taking tea with him, but he didn't order me out … How did you fellas get on?'

'I pretended I was a patent medicine rep when I was in the Carolinas last year,' Washburn said. 'Now I am notionally an aide to Sedgwick, and like you, nobody's queried it. Nat?'

'I was in the peninsular before the ban came into force, and when it did, I stayed close to those who trusted me.'

'I'll tell you what,' Richardson said, 'Halleck's ban really made me a passionate believer in the right to report, especially when he insulted Whitelaw Reid and myself when we confronted him with our petition against his ban, signed by thirty correspondents back in the summer. He said he would send us news so long as we were *outside* the lines. He refused to withdraw the order, so we Bohemians withdrew. But Henry Villard and I continued to send news of the army to the *Tribune*. Reporters disguised themselves in all manner of ways to get in with the army – subterfuges, aides, weapon reps and medical attendants. Generals and officers who understand the value of a good press aided many of us. The banning order simply died of neglect, and here we are holding an editorial meeting under the commander-in-chief's nose!'

Richardson suddenly raised a hand, indicating that he had just remembered something. 'I almost forgot,' he said as he fished a *Tribune* from his pocket. 'There's a cracking editorial in yesterday's paper that connects with what you were telling me earlier, Nat, about conspiracies.' He opened the paper and quoted: 'The air in Washington is thick with treason ... Be warned of a conspiracy between the chiefs of the Rebel and Union armies to subvert the republic and establish a pro-slavery despotism on its ruins.'

As he folded the paper and returned it to his pocket he added: 'Later it accuses the *Herald* of urging General McClellan to disperse Congress with the bayonet, after the fashion of Cromwell and Bonaparte ... which only reinforces how vital it is that we get the news to New York as quickly as possible, and to get it there way before the *Herald* in particular, with all their fancy vehicles and reporters tripping over one another.'

And Richardson yawned the yawn of a man who has just ridden from Cincinnati.

'I guess you need sleep,' Washburn grinned at him. 'Well, we all do. I suggest that Mr Paige and myself give a brief resumé of what we've learned today and not concern ourselves with the morrow until we have a steer on how matters resolve themselves tonight on South Mountain. Besides, my latest communication from Gay tells me that John Evans is in the vicinity of Harper's Ferry, so we can all concentrate on what's happening here.'

He told them of his chance meeting with McClellan and relayed anecdotes from his notebook, including the death of General Reno on the bullet of a sharpshooter. When Reno was stretchered off the field he greeted his friend by saying, 'Hallo Sam, I'm dead. Yes, yes, I'm dead. Goodbye!' And he died moments later.

Paige gave a brief account of Franklin's day at Crampton's Gap before Richardson and he turned in.

A couple of hours later when Washburn was tipping a reliable dispatch rider to take his speculative words to the telegraph office in Washington, an exasperated Strother showed him McClellan's latest message to Halleck. 'Today's action has been a glorious victory,' it said. Washburn just had time to add a sentence: 'Last night General McClellan is thought to have sent news of his "glorious victory" to the war department'.

He prayed that whoever prepared his piece for print at the Rookery would grasp the significance of that boast.

9

Up the Creek

Wednesday, 17 September 1862, 3am, Joseph Poffenberger's farm

The roar of bombardment from the direction of Harper's Ferry ended Washburn's short night under the stars near the army's HQ. Stonewall Jackson's guns on Maryland and Loudoun Heights rudely shattered the peace by cannonading the Feds on Bolivar Heights. The racket ceased at eight o'clock when, according to an eye-witness, a Federal brigadier in best dress uniform rode out bearing a white flag to complete surrender formalities with 'the worst dressed, worst mounted, most faded and dingy looking general' he had ever seen anyone surrender to.

Washburn splashed his face in the nearby stream, sought coffee at the makeshift officers' mess to wash down his breakfast of hard tack, attempted to straighten the creases from his blue jacket and hung close to the cookhouse in the hope of running into Strother or Babcock, or any aide who would give him an advance on what he had learned before falling into slumber, the gist of which was that the garrison at Harper's had abandoned Maryland Heights. McClellan's reaction was to order the garrison to hold out to the extremity, imploring it to 'reoccupy the Maryland Heights with your whole force'.

Meanwhile General Franklin, whose men had taken Crampton's Gap and this morning would be looking out over Pleasant Valley, was ordered to occupy the territory and proceed to the aid of the besieged garrison. Paige, who had been with Franklin's forces for most of yesterday's assault, reckoned that Jackson and his Rebels were too numerous and too well positioned for Franklin to reach the ferry in time, if he reached it at all.

The gloom of losing the ferry arsenal was offset by news that the enemy had slipped away from Turner's Gap under cover of darkness. The Army of the Potomac's First, Second and Twelfth Corps had repelled Rebel cavalry during the small hours and were marching along the National Road in pursuit, while the Ninth Corps advanced through Fox's Gap on the Sharpsburg road. Washburn overheard Fighting Joe Hooker given credit for circulating citizens' reports that Lee admitted to being whipped and was heading for the Potomac fords. McClellan made sure that Strother showed his gleeful message to Halleck to the *Tribune*:

'I am hurrying everything forward to endeavor to press their retreat to utmost.'

To which Lincoln replied: 'Your dispatch of today received. God bless you and all with you; destroy the Rebel army if possible.'

The other piece of intelligence that bore through the Monday morning mist at McClellan's HQ was how the Union cavalry deprived Jackson's victorious fighting men of booty. A rider brought tidings that Colonel Benjamin Franklin 'Grimes' Davis and 13,000 of his New York cavalrymen had bolted from Harper's Ferry that last evening by crossing the Potomac on a bridge run up by pontoniers. 'They skirted round the base of Maryland Heights and took the winding road north toward Sharpsburg,' alleged the messenger. 'The sparks of horses' shoes striking the rocky road lit the cavalrymen's way in the blackness of the night. They're strung out over ten miles and headed for the Williamsport to Hagerstown turnpike,' he added breathlessly to anyone within earshot. Moreover, Davis's horsemen met a Rebel wagon train in the pitch dark and cheerily turned it around. It was not until daylight that the Rebel drivers found their escort to be Federal cavalry with pistols cocked.

Washburn stirred with the infantry, gathering up his notebooks, revolver, blanket, flasks of water and whiskey and satchel and followed the troops and supply trains up the road to yesterday's battlefield. This was war without romance, but war with stench. His nostrils filled with the nausea of death as he passed heaps of enemy dead spread over a quarter of a mile. Burial details moved in eerie silence among the bodies. A lieutenant who identified himself as George Washington Whitman, brother of the poet, sat mesmerized in his saddle. Washburn came to a halt beside him, gave his name but nothing more.

Eventually Whitman said: 'Sometimes you move the corner of a blanket to reveal a smile, but sometimes a ghastly wound, an expression of agony.'

After another interval, Whitman told of a farmer who had made $60 by pitching bodies into his well at a dollar a corpse before sealing it, turning a bad situation to his advantage.

Farther on came more evidence of carnage, this time of Federal soldiers mown down where they charged. By the end of the day Washburn's notebook would estimate casualties at 1,800 Feds and 2,300 Rebels. He also noted rumor in the ranks that General Lee had been wounded when visiting the front. 'Not much chance of Napoleon being injured at the front,' said a sergeant within Washburn's hearing. 'He never comes close to the battle.'

Washburn rode on through Turner's Gap and, while contemplating whether Lee had gone for the Potomac as McClellan expected him to do, came upon Hooker taking brandy and water in the saddle. The general struck a clean and trim figure, as if he'd just made his morning toilet at Willard's Hotel. Washburn bade him good morning and asked if he had any comment for the readers of the *Tribune*.

'We've just heard from that observation post,' gesturing in its direction, 'that the Rebels have formed a line of battle for a mile-and-a-half on the other side of Antietam Creek, a stream that meanders into the Potomac three miles or so to the south. There's a ridge along the far side of the creek, about a hundred fifty feet high. They're spread along it, though maybe they won't be by the time your paper is next printed.'

Washburn followed the general's eye to an escarpment edged by timbered hills and ravines, and he could just make out the steeples of Sharpsburg beyond, a town serving farmers whose corn stood head high, whose orchards hung heavy with fruit, and whose haylofts were bulging when armies with empty stomachs arrived.

Hooker led his troops through Turner's Gap and through Boonsboro, where McClellan appeared on the Keedysville road to cheers from the men. Keedysville was a good eight miles from the gap, and at three o'clock McClellan sent scouts to reconnoiter the terrain and Rebel positions ahead. Washburn made his own observations, noting that the land to the north of the town was flatter than to the south, and the patchwork of fields, woods, corn and thick foliage was peppered with rocky outcrops, small groves and dips and swells of rolling farmland.

Dismounting, Washburn studied his map for the twentieth time in the past few days. If your uniform was blue, five roads led to Sharpsburg. If you marched in pale gray, five roads led *from* the little town. For McClellan, a turnpike headed south from Hagerstown and Pennsylvania, another ran southwest from

Boonsboro and the National Road, and roads ran westwards from Rohrersville and north from Harper's Ferry. For Lee, the only practicable Potomac crossing point between Harper's Ferry and Williamsport was Boteler's Ford, a long way upstream. The three miles of road to Boteler's was his only escape route to Virginia.

The creek in the foreground was just wide and deep enough to hinder wagons and artillery. Four arched stone bridges spanned it – the first where it joined the Potomac, Lower Bridge where the road to Rohrbach and Harper's Ferry crossed the creek, Middle Bridge carrying the Boonsboro turnpike and Upper Bridge near Samuel Pry's gristmill to the north, where the road from Keedysville to Williamsport crossed Antietam Creek. Pry's Ford lay between the Middle and Upper Bridges.

Washburn's map confirmed that Lee had only one way out of Maryland. If he was going to stay and fight, he had chosen his ground well. But Washburn would put a stack of bills on McClellan interpreting the Rebel battle line as a bluff by Lee's rear guard to ease his retreat to the river, as set out in the general's original instructions in 'lost' Order 191.

These thoughts ended abruptly when a Rebel battery opened fire, causing the Union generals to abandon their survey and scatter. In the safety of Keedysville, word came from McClellan that the opportunity to attack this day had passed, and his scouts reported that Jackson was on the road from Harper's Ferry to Sharpsburg. Another precious gift of time from McClellan to Lee, Washburn noted.

The rest of the day was frenetic. Army headquarters moved to Pry's farm and teamsters jammed roads and lanes with endless ordnance, quartermaster, commissary and ambulance trains. Skirmishers found hides from where to eye Rebels on the bluffs.

Pinkerton agents and cavalry scouts slipped over the creek to ascertain if Lee was coming or going, and Washburn, to his relief, found Paige and Richardson. 'We'll make a plan as soon as we can find out what Young Napoleon has in mind,' he told his fellow *Tribune* correspondents.

The answer to the Lee question was 'coming'. As the evening wore on, increasing numbers of the men who had taken Harper's Ferry were seen in the vicinity of Sharpsburg. As the *Tribune* men prepared to turn in, Washburn decreed that they should rendezvous at nightfall next day close to McClellan's headquarters, and every nightfall until action ceased.

'I assume Evans will send something over on the fall of Harper's tonight, and I'll send a few paragraphs on McClellan's inaction. Meanwhile, keep an eye on what the other scribes are up to. I saw Villard cursing earlier today when the *Herald*'s horses put their carriage in a ditch!'

Just then, Washburn caught somebody's eye over the shoulders of Paige and Richardson, and continued: 'And Charlie Coffin from the *Boston Journal* has just got in, good man, but we don't have to worry about him like we do the *Herald* or *Times*.'

Coffin, having exchanged his editor's desk to ride with the Bohemians, came over to shake him by the hand.

'Just got here from Parkton, Maryland, via Hanover Junction, Westminster, Harrisburg and Greencastle. My plan was to ride south and observe the fight from Lee's fiefdom, but I was warned that I'd never pass for a Confed sympathizer, so here I am. How's Young Napoleon doing?' And they compared notes until yawns won the night.

At daybreak on Tuesday, General McClellan set Pry's farm abuzz by deploying his forces along the eastern side of the brown and sluggish creek. His plan, Strother told Washburn, was to probe both of Lee's flanks. Hooker's corps would go north to the Upper Bridge between the forks of the Big and Little Antietam. Sumner's corps was to his left near the Middle Bridge and Burnside's near the Lower Bridge. By noon Mansfield's Twelfth Corps had arrived, bringing McClellan's divisions to thirty-five against estimates of fourteen on the Rebel side.

The plan seemed sound enough, but to Washburn its execution was 'miserable from beginning to end' as he noted some time later. Hours were soaked up reconnoitering enemy positions, examining ground, finding fords, clearing approaches and hurrying artillery and supply trains. There was something leisurely about the deployment of the Army of the Potomac's infantry and artillery, as if McClellan once again had no intention of doing battle this day.

At noon, First Corps had made no move, while Ninth Corps was ordered to take up positions near Lower Bridge, but did not march until three o'clock. Meanwhile, the guns on the heights above and below Middle Bridge – guns superior in weight, calibration, range and number to the obsolete iron pieces and small calibers at Lee's disposal – did much damage to Rebel troops gathering on high ground near the tiny white Dunker Church, a place of worship for a pacifist sect that had become a rallying point for Jackson's men. Whenever a Rebel moved, a Union gun roared. Retaliation soon ceased because the gunners in gray were short of ammunition.

When Hooker's corps stirred, McClellan summoned Fightin' Joe and ordered him – by dictation to Strother's immaculate hand – to cross Antietam Creek and turn toward Sharpsburg. At last urgency was in the air, and Washburn determined to stay close, reasoning that if there were action, Hooker would be at the heart of it.

'What else is afoot?' he asked Strother.

'No orders have been issued, nor has he met the corps commanders, but I overheard him boast that he will "pinch him up in a vice". As I say, that means crossing the Lower Bridge to confront the Rebel southern flank, and attacking Lee's center when the flanks are engaged. No time to do all that today, I guess.'

Armed with what looked like a strategy, Washburn directed Paige to follow Burnside, the new boy at the head of his corps, and Richardson to stay with Sumner in the center, while he shadowed Hooker. As he spurred off, he called for rendezvous at the Pry house when darkness fell. 'If that's not possible, we'll try again on the morrow.'

By four o'clock Hooker's columns were snaking over Upper Bridge or splashing through Pry's Ford and swinging north and west through fields and woodlots to reach Hagerstown turnpike to the Rebel left. The cavalry went ahead to reconnoiter and shots broke out from a Rebel battery.

Hooker himself rode out front with two regiments of skirmishers. When a long line of men in gray emerged from the trees with muskets blazing, a shell sent Washburn's horse rearing, and he followed Hooker's lead of hurdling a fence to get out of range.

Much to the reporter's surprise, McClellan appeared on the field, presenting Hooker with the opportunity to opine loudly that, having lost a thousand men at Turner's Gap, 'If I don't get reinforcements against the entire Rebel army, I will be eaten up.'

While he could still see to write, Washburn noted that McClellan squandered another chance of catching Lee on the hop by moving Hooker's corps in broad daylight. He might just as well have 'telegraphed his punch', as someone said of his tactics on South Mountain. A Rebel division awaited Hooker's men on the Smoketown Road, and artillery blasted the Feds on both sides as light faded.

Hooker ordered the Third and the Thirteenth Pennsylvania Reserves – the Bucktails – to advance to a plowed field on Samuel Poffenberger's farm. When they emerged into the open, artillery and small arms fire raked them from the East Woods. They were compelled to throw themselves flat in the furrowed field to avoid death or injury. The tactic of repeated dives over plowed waves took them as far as the fence, where the Rebels confronted them until the light faded and the fight died in darkness.

'We are through for tonight, gentlemen,' Hooker remarked, 'but tomorrow we fight the battle that will decide the fate of the republic.'

The night was not to relish. Fires were banned, and so sustenance was restricted to chewing on hard tack and coffee grinds, but at least they were better off than the starving, straggling and shoeless Rebel troops who, according to Federal scouts, had few supplies and were forced to live on foraged pumpkins, green corn, apples and cider. The news that Harper's Ferry had fallen to Jackson was no comfort to a Rebel suffering a dose of Virginia quickstep.

From Poffenberger's barn where Hooker had set up headquarters, Washburn shadowed the general's visit to his picket line in the East Woods, where he dismounted and crept close enough to hear the enemy talking. Back at the barn, news came that Joseph Mansfield's Twelfth Corps and five batteries of artillery had crossed the creek and were bivouacked a mile or so to the rear. Unluckily for them, their camp was on a field that had been freshly manured.

At two o'clock rain was falling. Washburn dozed fitfully beneath a tree near the entrance to the barn, his bridle anchored round an arm and his blanket and mackintosh meager defense against sporadic drizzle. Waves of anticipation and anxiety ebb and flowed through his mind as the biggest fight that either army had ever seen was about to take place; a clash of cause against belief. Thousands of souls wrestled with fear of defeat and fear of cowardice as they lay half awake in sodden fields and woods surrounding Sharpsburg.

Washburn played over scraps of conversation he had had with Bucktails in the last few hours. 'The truth is,' one said to him, 'that far from eager to be led against the enemy, when bullets are whacking against tree trunks and solid shot is cracking skulls like eggshells, the consuming passion in the breast of the average man is "get out of the way". Between the physical fear of going forward and the moral fear of turning back, now there's a predicament of exceptional awkwardness. But,' the soldier continued, 'when the order came to go forward, we did not falter. In a second the air was hissing with bullets and hurtling grapeshot. The mental strain was so great that the whole landscape for an instant turned slightly red.'

'If I lose my life,' another said, 'I shall be missed but by few; but if the Union or Confederation be lost, it will be missed by many'.

All about were men prepared to die while convincing themselves that they would not. Some scribbled letters in the dark, including Washburn's Bostonian acquaintance Oliver Wendell Holmes Jr, a lieutenant in the Twentieth Massachusetts, who had shown him what he wrote to his parents before entrusting it to the army mail: 'It's rank folly pulling a long mug every time one may fight or may be killed. Very probably we shall in a few days and if we do, why, I shall go into it not trying to shirk the responsibility of my past life ...'

Drizzle and restlessness marked the night. By three o'clock fighting had long ceased, but sudden bursts of artillery periodically shattered sleep. Jittery shots spattered from picket lines. Someone tripped over a dog and fell onto a stack of rifles, waking two regiments. Firing sprang up again, and Hooker rose at once. Rapid picket shots gave way to heavy volleys. The general listened a moment and smiled grimly. 'We have no troops there. The Rebels are shooting each other!'

So everybody lay down again, and as Hooker returned to his camp bed he rasped to an underling that 'if they had let us start earlier, we might have finished tonight.' Washburn repeated the dictum to himself to plant it in his memory.

There were frequent alarms all the short night through. Washburn finally dozed off in the arms of Ida, whose letter was warmly close to his breast in his innermost pocket.

10

Battle Joined at Antietam

Wednesday, 17 September 1862, late afternoon at Pry's farm
When Washburn awoke at five o'clock, General Hooker was already in the saddle, immaculate and clean-shaven, issuing orders to his units. The rain had stopped, and troops with primed Enfields and Springfields pushed forward into the mist. They advanced through the North Woods on either side of the Hagerstown pike into a field of ripe, head high corn. Washburn, fortified by a piece of hardtack soaked in brandy, attached himself to Hooker's entourage. The mist soon lifted to reveal a warm, bright morning where golden sunbeams bounced off bayonets in the corn. Beyond the junction of Smoketown Road and Hagerstown pike stood the glowing white steeple of Dunker Church.

Stonewall Jackson and the Rebels lay in wait. Long-range guns detonated every other second, pounding woods and fields to destruction.

Fighting Joe, with his prominent nose and flushed face, rode along the firing line on his white charger. He gazed on strife as if it were a stage set with himself as director, barking instructions to the cast and dispatching spear carriers on errands: 'Order that man to the rear. Order that regiment to move their backsides.' Washburn sat quietly on horseback in the grand circle, watching the drama unfold. Just as he imagined a naked Ida Godiva to gallop up to claim her prince and save the day, Hooker, his staff now all disbursed on errands, beckoned. Looking Washburn straight in the eye, he demanded: 'Who are you?'

'Special correspondent of the New York *Tribune*, sir.'

'Will you take an order for me? Tell the colonel of that regiment to take his men to the front and keep them there.'

Washburn spurred off in the direction of Hooker's gesture and reined in beside the colonel, who looked him up and down in vain search for insignia. The reporter relayed the general's command, word for word.

'Who are you?'

'The order is General Hooker's, sir.'

'It must come to me from a staff officer or from my brigade commander.'

'Very good, sir. I shall report to General Hooker that you decline to obey.'

Washburn made to turn his horse.

'Oh for God's sake, don't do that. The Rebels are too many for us, but I should rather face them than Hooker.'

And the colonel summoned an orderly to set his regiment moving.

When Washburn reported back, Hooker said: 'Don't let the next one talk so much.'

Thus Fighting Joe engaged the *Tribune* correspondent to carry out many more missions that morning.

After two hours of fierce fighting, it was evident that the kernel of the battleground was farmer Miller's twenty-four-acre cornfield. From dawn, the First Corps had engaged in a deadly struggle with Rebel artillery and infantry. A plowed field, Miller's cornfield and woodlots stretched away toward more fields and more Rebel positions, a battle canvas like a promontory jutting into the ocean. Washburn's errands took him hither and thither as the line of fire swayed first one way, then to the other. Hooker was never away from the fire. Two-thirds of his men were Pennsylvania veterans of Manassas, and the reporter noted that they fought with a will.

Half an hour into intense fighting, the Rebels began to weaken. The Feds broke into a cheering rush, and the enemy retreated through the cornfield to the woods, abandoning dead and wounded. The Pennsylvanians followed until a volley smote their front line, hurling them back over half the distance they had gained. Washburn's heart raced, and not for the first time did he catch a fleeting image of galloping Ida, snug under his shirt. As he focused his glasses on First Corps he heard a metallic ding and felt a stabbing pain at his side. A sharpshooter's ball had struck his water flask, singed his coat and grazed his thigh. He dismounted, calmed his horse, recovered the spent missile and drank from the dented but still intact flask. 'Hasten to safer ground,' whispered Ida in his ear.

The fortune of the day had turned in the space of ten minutes. Endless lines of Rebels now swept into the cornfield from where their comrades had just fled. Hooker, his center in danger of annihilation, called up the nearest brigade, and when it failed to make ground, dispatched Washburn to his second-in-command with the order to 'give me your best brigade instantly.'

The brigade duly arrived in the corn to face a hail of shot and shells. The veterans stood their ground while stragglers from the previous onslaught retreated from Rebel fire.

Hooker turned to Washburn and said: 'I think they will hold it.'

As he spoke, regiments from Massachusetts pushed forward and sent Rebel forces fleeing to the woods for the second time that morning. 'Gallant', 'determined', 'heroic fighting', 'desperate day' were scribbled into Washburn's notebook.

At seven o'clock General Mansfield's Twelfth Corps swept

into the East Wood. Washburn wondered what took Mansfield so long. He was several hours behind Hooker in joining the fight, and there was yet no sign of Sumner's Second Corps. Goodness knows what was happening on Burnside's flank. Meanwhile Lee, having blocked Hooker's forces, was free to move his men to his left flank as the sun climbed higher, thanks to McClellan's failure to coordinate an attack. Now there was stalemate. The Rebels were too extended to be turned but too strong to be broken.

Rebel guns poured a galling enfilading fire into Hooker's central line for half an hour before the general announced his determination to take the woods beyond the cornfield. To Washburn's surprise his maneuver had an audience, for several thousand good people of Sharpsburg had gathered on a neighboring hillside to watch the struggle.

The *Tribune* man was aghast to see Hooker ride out ahead of his front line, dismount and continue on foot to survey the ground for placement of a battery. The commander behaved in such cavalier fashion often, riding without a staff officer or orderly nearby, oblivious to enemy muskets and readily visible on the field. He was a sniper's sitting duck, for sure. Washburn had even tried to tell him so, but failed to get his message across. He held his breath as the general re-mounted in the midst of a fresh volley. Hooker had not ridden five steps before a ball struck his foot. He remained swaying in the saddle as he barked orders:

'There is a regiment to the right,' he hollered. 'Order it forward! Tell them to carry these woods and hold them – and it is our fight.'

Aides caught Hooker as he fell. Curses poured from his mouth and blood from his leg. The field surgeon announced that the bullet had passed right through the general's foot without breaking a bone. Hooker might well think that his own part of the battle was won as orderlies carted him away and cheers rang out from the ranks. After fighting had raged for eight hours, Hooker's right flank was untouched and his center line was making progress.

General Sumner arrived to assume command. He rode bareheaded through the trees with a veteran's confidence, far ahead of his leading brigade. Gray hair and gray whiskers set off the fire in his eyes. His column, together with General Sedgwick's division, plunged straight into the confusing fray. Washburn watched as the Thirty-Fourth New York's color party was shot to pieces. Balls hit Sedgwick himself in the shoulder, leg and wrist. Despite his injuries he persisted in remaining on the field so long as there was a chance of saving it.

Washburn drew back and dismounted by a stream to take stock and allow his horse to drink. For the first time his body complained of being on the go since first light. He allowed himself a biscuit and nips of brandy between gulps of water. The situation that was running in the Feds' favor when Hooker was carried away shifted to favor the Confeds after Mansfield was injured and Sedgwick was stretchered away. Hooker's troops were exhausted, Mansfield's were no better, and Sumner's command had taken heavy losses. Added to that, the Federal batteries that kept the Rebels at bay were running short of ammunition.

From his vantage point Washburn could hear heightening commotion in the west, emanating from the arrival of Franklin's Sixth Corps from Pleasant Valley. They soon swept the Rebels out of the cornfield and the surrounding woods once again. After this, the incessant cannonade ceased. Staff officers were jittery until pickets reported no signs of Rebel movement. Both armies were exhausted.

Eventually McClellan and Strother appeared on an inspection

tour. The commander showed no sign of recognizing Washburn, but the latter sensed that Strother was licensed to pass information to the *Tribune*. Strother muttered that Sumner could hold his position but not advance without reinforcements, and Burnside had yet to get all of his corps across the Lower Bridge. Aggressive fire from the slopes had met the troops who *had* crossed the creek.

Washburn's analysis had McClellan covering himself against failure. He decided to go and find Burnside in the cause of assembling as complete a picture of the day as possible and getting it to New York by any possible means for *Tribune* readers. He should also cover himself in case he, Richardson and Paige failed to meet later. God only knows where Evans had gotten.

He rode across the creek at Pry's Ford, his way taking him close to McClellan's HQ, when a most extraordinary thing happened. A staff officer galloped up, gave his name as Lieutenant Wilson, and suggested that Washburn should ask Hooker to take command of the army.

'Most of us think that this battle is only half fought and half won,' Wilson said uneasily. 'There is still time to finish it, but McClellan will do no more.'

Washburn was speechless, pointing out that such a move would be an act of mutiny in the presence of the enemy.

'I know it, you know it, we all know it, but we know also that it is the only way to crush Lee and end the rebellion and save the country,' Wilson replied.

After much parleying, Washburn consented to visit Fighting Joe to inquire of his condition. He found Hooker in bed in a little redbrick house, suffering great pain but perking up when enquiring eagerly for news of the battle. On hearing that no progress had been made during the last two hours, the general expressed anger in no uncertain terms. As he spoke plainly of McClellan, Washburn seized the opportunity to ask if his wound would permit him to mount again that day.

'No, it is impossible.'

'Or take command of your corps from a carriage?'

'No, no, I cannot move. I'm perfectly helpless. The pain is bad enough, but what I hate to think is that it was a Rebel bullet that did it.'

Washburn told him that McClellan was resting on his laurels and would not engage his reserves, and there was every prospect of Lee escaping. 'Unless,' he continued.

Hooker sensed the hidden purpose of the question.

'You need not go on. You must see I cannot move. But who sent you here?'

Washburn said that the situation was critical and some of the general's friends were anxious to know if he could resume his duties in an emergency. Hooker groaned and swore and tried to raise himself on the bed, without success. The attendant surgeon caught Washburn's eye and shook his head vigorously. When the general repeated his question, Washburn excused himself, promising to squash the scheme brewing among the headquarters staff, and to return when he was able.

After reporting his conversation to Wilson, Washburn picked his way past ambulances and supply wagons along the Boonsboro pike before cutting across country to Rohrbach and the neck of Burnside's operation at Lower Bridge. The ride was glorious under the splendor of a clear September sky, a blue heaven that capped a veil of white smoke enveloping hilltops, ridges and woods along four miles of battlefront. The fate of the republic hung on the hour. Despite the butchery and suffering, Washburn warmed to the grandeur of the day and the significance of the moment.

It was past three o'clock when he arrived at Burnside's Bridge to observe the slow advance up the slopes on the west side of the creek. Batteries in the rear covered the movement of the infantry. Rebel guns were also in full play, and a desperate fight raged in a deep ravine to the right, while heavy columns of Rebel troops could be seen, careless of concealment, advancing over the hills toward Burnside's forces.

Washburn watched Burnside's guns silence Rebel batteries on the hilltops. Dark lines of infantry moved rapidly and steadily upwards, plainly visible against the green backdrop. The reporter followed, and was composing a colorful account when clouds of dust suddenly canopied the road and covered the mêlée of wagons, guns, horses and men in the valley below. Flashes of blue smoke from a Rebel gun burst among them, causing men and horses to go down. But the dark blue whirlwind swept on, too close for Washburn's comfort, despite his surprising coolness under fire earlier in the day. A bullet whistled past his head and two grazed his horse, who whinnied loudly and almost threw him.

The Feds carried the hill, but could they hold it? Washburn retreated to a vantage point where he could calm his horse. Another Rebel battle line appeared on the ridge, unleashing a tempest of shell on to Burnside's men. A second line followed and moved swiftly down in perfect order. Despite being met by incessant discharges of Fed musketry, the Rebels did not fire a shot. The line of bayonets instantly closed white spaces where men fell, and the line continued its advance. The Feds showed no sign of giving way. Washburn could hardly believe what he saw, feasting his eyes on such bravery, such courage, such resolve, such carnage. The Rebel left flank suddenly scattered over the field while the rest stood fast. Burnside was outnumbered, outflanked and compelled to yield the hill so boldly taken. The general had lost the initiative.

From where he stood, Washburn could see Burnside's bivouac and what was now referred to as 'Burnside's Bridge'. A two-horse wagon advertising the 'New York Daguerreian Miniature Gallery' waited its turn to cross the creek, and when it did so, he inquired of the photographer and his assistant how they were faring in the battle.

'Well sir, we have robust cameras and a portable dark room to make pictures by the wet-plate collodion method, but of course keeping up with the army is a slow and tedious business. I am appointed to the staff of General McClellan with the honorary rank of captain – Captain Alexander Gardner at your service – a position that harbors as many disadvantages as advantages. The army only wants pictures that show it in heroic light.'

Washburn had never given thought to photography outside the portrait studio, but his brief meeting with Captain Gardner made him realize that the camera, unlike the brush of a *Harper's* artist, doesn't lie. Artists usually depict order, color, patriotism and moral sanctity to adorn the hearths of western homesteads, courtesy of illustrated magazines and prints from Messrs Currier & Ives.

Presently a rider galloped away toward McClellan's HQ, and the reporter waved the wet-plate master goodbye as he pursued the messenger as quickly as his limping horse could carry him. It was a good wager that Burnside was asking for the engagement of Fitz John Porter's fresh Fifth Corps, the reserve force idling the hours away in the valley below. Washburn loped up the farm lane just in time to see the messenger salute McClellan and Porter and read out Burnside's cryptic missive: 'I want troops and guns. If you do not send them I cannot hold my position for half an hour.'

Porter muttered something to McClellan, who shook his head, glanced at the western sky, and said nothing for a while. Washburn bet that McClellan was about to fight shy of committing his remaining reserves. Young Napoleon turned to the rider and spoke very slowly: 'Tell General Burnside that this is the battle of the war. He must hold his ground till dark at any cost. I will send him Miller's battery. I can do nothing more. I have no infantry.'

As the messenger spurred off, McClellan called him back.

'Tell him if he *cannot* hold his ground, then the bridge, to the last man! *Always the bridge!* If the bridge is lost, all is lost.'

11

Washburn's Bohemian Ride

Saturday, 20 September 1862, 6am at 152 Nassau, Manhattan

Darkness dropped a pall of silence over the hinterland of Sharpsburg, broken only by whinnies, clumping hoofs and the distant wail of a harmonica. Miraculously, the four *Tribune* men found each other at Pry's farm. Richardson, who had procured a canteen of lobscouse, led them to the far end of an empty barn. They huddled at a table in the corner and passed the canteen round, a banquet of salt pork and hard tack boiled with goodness knows what. While they ate, stretcher cases were carried into the barn and set down in rows. 'My God, I thought this was too good to be true,' Richardson said. 'We're in a field hospital.'

'Keep your heads down,' Washburn replied, 'for the chances of finding another place to parley are nil. There was no escape from the carnage on the field, for even now Gardner will be up to his elbows in his wet-plate collodion wagon transforming images captured by his lenses into stereographs for posterity. On the contrary, the talented men with brush and sketchpad will be shaping the patriotism of Young Napoleon and his gallant Union army on colorful fields of glory.'

The correspondents began their discussion in the flicker of a tallow candle. Flasks of coffee, whiskey and brandy served as relief against the odors of medicament as much as to quench thirst. Farmyard smells soon gave way to wafts of chloroform and ether, and the screams of victims of the sawbones' black art pierced the quiet.

Washburn began by throwing doubt on the general assumption that action would re-start in the morning because the day's fighting was inconclusive. 'Who knows,' he queried, 'whether Lee or McClellan have the stomach for more slaughter, when the one can run for the Potomac and the other need only sit and watch.

'McClellan has been showing customary caution, some would say cowardice, since he took South Mountain,' he said, 'and I wager he'll dither tomorrow while reassuring the high command in Washington that victory is at hand. So we must get an account of what happened today to the Rookery as soon as possible as well as prime our readers for victory, defeat, chaos or truce on the morrow. My intention is to summarize what each of us has seen and take it to New York personally, for I don't trust any telegraph or Wells Fargo outfit to deliver it directly without diverting it to Washington's eyes. Which is why I must take another horse, for mine's suffered a couple of hits and is too lame to undertake a long ride, poor beast. My proud blue coat took punishment too,' and he indicated a large rip from the whistling bullet that dented his flask. 'Al,' he continued, looking directly at Richardson, 'can we call you Al? In my absence you're in charge of who writes on what to send to Gay. Don't forget that Thomson may return from New York in time to be useful.'

He took a long draft of coffee. For a minute or two the four men glanced round their grief-ridden meeting place, alone with their own thoughts. A striking woman was distributing bandages and lanterns to orderlies and ladling gruel into bowls from a huge cooking pot to feed casualties. Washburn was aghast at the casual attitude of the army surgeons and the lack of hygiene. Better to die than be wounded in battle, he thought to himself. And better still to get on with the business in hand. He called the meeting to attention.

'I'll give you a summary of my day and then we'll go round the table.'

Washburn recounted the optimistic telegrams McClellan sent to Halleck anticipating the destruction of the enemy, and how his claims belied Little Mac's leisurely pace of deploying his hundred thousand men for battle. He told them of Hooker's eve of battle move and fighting spirit, his courage and his frustration with McClellan. He told them of ebb and flow over plowed fields, through woods and tangled in the mature cornfields, of the wounding of Hooker and Mansfield, of assault by battery, of artillery shells raking open fields. He told them of his shocking surprise on seeing hundreds, maybe thousands, of folk from Sharpsburg gathered on a hilltop to watch the action. He recounted his ride to Burnside's flank and General Burnside's vain appeal for reinforcements when he could see Porter's infantry and Pleasonton's cavalry held back in reserve.

'I've seen nothing of the struggle in the center or the south apart from a distant sight of Burnside's men clearing Rebels off the ridge overlooking the bridge that crosses the creek. So,' turning to Richardson, 'Al, where have you been these last twelve hours?'

'I concentrated on making friends with officers and getting to know the terrain after the long ride from Washington, well, from the west. I heard plenty of dissension over McClellan's handling of his army. What struck me was that corps commanders were kept waiting for orders interminably. While McClellan was out reconnoitering, I saw Sumner sitting under a tree, Hooker dozing on the grass, and Burnside chattering with his staff. Napoleon should have had them in the field long before if he was to live up to his name. I visited batteries in the hills to get an idea of firepower. I contemplated trying to go behind the enemy lines on Hooker's flank, but decided against. Too dangerous. I'm not crazy like you, George – can we call you George? – galloping around after Fightin' Joe.'

Washburn did not rise to the jibe. 'Better write something about that, what you saw from the batteries or wherever you got to,' he said.

'Sure, but then I went back to where Burnside's troops were assaulting the ridge and arrived in time to see a shell score a direct hit on a Rebel caisson and explode it. I've already written something on that, and have a copy for you.'

He handed a sheet to Washburn, who scanned it as best he could in the light of the lamp: '… riderless horses, scattering men, clouds of dirt, exploding shells, lines of infantry swaying to and fro, smoke from muskets, red flashes and white puffs from batteries, sun shining on scene of tumult …'

Richardson glanced round the table.

'I certainly share George's anxiety about McClellan's tactics, if not his strategy. There will surely be chagrin and disappointment if he fails to follow through tomorrow. He will lose his army's respect and he'll sink his ambition to live in the White House. I truly wonder what Abe Lincoln's thinking.'

'Thanks, Al,' Washburn said, pausing to take another drink before asking John Evans – should we call you Johnnie? – to describe his most recent twenty-four hours. A hint of a smile passed Washburn's lips as he recalled hearing Evans described as a 'whiskered goat'. Evans saw the sign and began to stroke his beard.

'I was grazing in Pleasant Valley with Franklin's troops yesterday to assess the Rebels' rout of Harper's Ferry,' and he scanned his notes:

'Jackson's men freed a Midas of treasure. About eleven

thousand five hundred men of the garrison were paroled, thirteen hundred small arms were requisitioned, two hundred wagons, abundant supplies and seventy-three pieces of artillery. Each side had suffered about two hundred casualties.'

He looked up, and continued, 'The best thing from our point of view was that the Rebels' anticipation of fresh mounts and new cavalry equipment melted away during their night of victory when Colonel Davis's troopers – as many as thirteen hundred, I heard – slipped away to Pennsylvania. Their breakout was enough to vex a saint. Nevertheless, the needy Confeds picked Harper's Ferry clean. They pilloried supply depots and sutlers wagons for anything to eat or wear. Men without guns obtained guns, and regiments with old smoothbores re-equipped themselves with rifled Springfields. A Fed soldier told me that Jackson appeared "seedy and dirty like his barefoot troops, wearing an old hat that a Northern beggar would have passed up". He paused for breath. 'But if Jackson had been one of ours, we wouldn't have been caught in this trap.'

'There was no chance of relieving the ferry?' Washburn asked.

'No. Franklin was bivouacked at Crampton's Gap and received contradictory, or at best vague orders from McClellan. He was told to take Pleasant Valley, relieve Harper's Ferry and march north to Boonsboro. The valley was already awash with Rebels. Later he received a message which I got to see and write down: "Drive enemy in your front, but be cautious in doing it until you have some idea of his force. Thus far our success is complete, but let us follow it up closely, but warily." Franklin was also supposed to send a division to Rohrersville to guard the army's back. While his orders piled up, he received no response to his call for additional troops. I overheard a shouted exchange across no-man's-land in which a Rebel soldier reported that the ferry had been taken. It came as news to Franklin, I think.'

'Well done, Johnnie,' Washburn said. 'It seems McClellan sowed confusion rather than sense there. Unless he had poor intelligence. But when he has good intelligence, he usually chooses to ignore it.'

'That's true enough,' Evans said. 'In the afternoon I rode with Franklin's men and found Burnside at the bridge, but I was too late to see anything much happening.'

Washburn turned to Nathaniel Paige. 'What, pray, have you uncovered in the last twenty-four hours, Nat?'

'I had an extraordinary conversation by chance last night,' Paige said. 'McClellan's judge advocate was staying in the same house, I have his name somewhere,' shuffling his notes, 'Major John J Key. He clearly wanted to unburden himself, and launched into what he had told me a few days before, that morale among the officers was extremely low, and McClellan's staff had held a conference where most declared that they had lost faith in the administration and military leaders who kept on losing battles...'

'What's new about this since you first heard it?' Washburn asked.

'I guess only that there's been a meeting. Key said that the argument was going in favor of setting up a military dictatorship until he, by his own account, remonstrated and broke the meeting up without a conclusion. There's obviously something going on, and I think we should keep an eye on it. It squares with what you say about McClellan,' he said, glancing up at Washburn.

Washburn nodded agreement and remarked that he had heard something of that from his best contact on McClellan's staff. He decided not to share his part in the appeal to Hooker to usurp

McClellan, and turned the discussion back to the day's action.

'Where have you been on the field, Nat?'

'I have a reasonably up-to-date list of dead and wounded officers,' came the answer.

'Never mind that,' Washburn replied. 'What action have you witnessed? Where have you been under fire?'

Paige fidgeted in his chair. Then he said: 'Forget not the old but true adage that names sell newspapers, even if they are the names of the dead, so my time has not been wasted.' Pause. 'For part of the day I was exposed to cannonading, but I do not think it the duty of correspondents to expose their lives under musketry fire when there is nothing to be gained by it. I saw nothing to be gained.'

Washburn remembered Hill's character reference for Paige: 'Not good at battle reporting, nor does he take kindly to taking orders. The *Trib* hired Paige because he was a promising writer.' What Washburn had just heard incensed him.

'You're here to get close to the army and report battles, not to compile lists of casualties,' he shouted, rising from his chair. Paige half stood and recoiled.

'I didn't receive any instructions from you as *Tribune* chief-of-staff all day,' he snapped. 'It's all very well running errands for army staff, but my humble opinion is that your job is to pay attention to *Tribune* staff, not service the army.'

Both men were on their feet with fists raised when the whiskered goat sprang up and exclaimed, 'Gentlemen, gentlemen, we're all *Tribune* men with a long day in the field behind us … and a job to do …'

Richardson smiled and remarked that the hour was late, nerves were running high, and perhaps they should sit down and pool their information instead of worrying about what might have been. 'It's a war, for God's sake, a senseless eruption that we are charged with making some sense of!'

'We mustn't allow trivialities to divert our minds as the earth trembles with events that shape our destinies,' Evans added.

At that point the tenor strains of *When This Cruel War Is Over* floated up from the far end of the barn, as if to reinforce the wisdom of the goat, and the Bohemians settled down again to the task in hand.

It was approaching midnight when Washburn finished collating notes and mounted Richardson's horse to ride twenty-five miles to Frederick. They had weighed up the possibilities of finding a telegraph connection at Hagerstown or Frederick, and settled on the latter. They knew that the battle at the creek had outrun the field telegraph service, for the men who strung wires across country worked at a miserable pace of two miles per hour, and remained some distance away. The army's messages were sent to Harrisburg via Hagerstown by courier and relayed to Washington via Baltimore. Frederick was a better bet for a rail connection even if its telegraph turned out to be defunct. But Washburn might have to ride all the way to New York, on a strange horse, an empty stomach and without prospect of sleep.

The moonlit road took him through Boonsboro and Turner's Gap to Middletown, and he reduced the beast's canter to a lope as he dozed fitfully in the saddle, checking now and then that the horse was on course while composing passages of reportage in his head. He was dog tired and ravenous, but adrenaline was the only available nourishment. Besides, the awe of responsibility for releasing news of the war's most important battle to date and putting it into print before anybody else reminded him constantly of the purpose of his night ride.

Shortly after three o'clock, before sun up, Washburn rode into Frederick's deserted streets that were festooned with Union flags, limp in the still air. There was no sign of life at the ticket office or the telegraph office at the Baltimore and Ohio's depot. He tethered Richardson's horse to a bench and fell into fitful slumber, to be woken some time later by a waft of coffee.

He found the stationmaster sipping the brew in his office.

'Good day to you, sir. Do you know when the telegraph opens?'

'Don't know nothing of the telegraph. There's an operator, but whether he can operate, I don't know. He don't start 'til later, seven or after,' all the while staring into his fire.

'And when's the next train to Baltimore?'

'If a steamer or a caboose shows up any time today, I'll eat my hat. One might go at any moment, or not at all. You'll have to take your chances, what with the military requisitioning everything and all.'

'If that's the situation, can you charter me an iron horse to get me to Baltimore?'

What gave him hope was the sight of steam rising from the engine house down the track.

'You need a military warrant to hire a train. McClellan's rules. It's more than my life's worth to deviate from the instruction.'

'Then please ask the war department to permit General Hooker's aide-de-camp to requisition a train as soon as your operative arrives.'

'Yes sir – *if* the operative arrives.' The mention of Hooker had made a mark.

'And may I purchase a cup of your fine coffee?'

'No sir. But it would be my honor to take coffee with an aide to Fighting Joe Hooker!'

And he handed Washburn a mug of steaming brew.

'I appreciate it, sir.'

The reporter left the stationmaster's den and led his horse to water and fodder at the livery now awaking across the street. He hunched on his bench to contemplate continuing in the saddle to Baltimore, where the railroad connects directly with New York. But just as he resigned himself to ride on, a figure wearing a hat proclaiming 'American Telegraph Co' arrived at the telegraph office. After some demur, which seemed to be a characteristic of Frederick folk, the ATC man condescended to transmit a short message.

Sending half a dozen sheets of synopsis from the meeting at the farm risked interception by the war department or the White House, so Washburn scribbled a couple of terse passages addressed to Gay at the Rookery signaling, in the language of a hop bitters salesman, that the Army of the Potomac had narrowly won a bloodthirsty stalemate against Lee's forces at Sharpsburg, and was poised 'to push the Rebels back into Virginia today if General McClellan chooses so to do.' He concluded by saying that he hoped to deliver a full account of the battle that night. And please oblige by acknowledging this message.

Before the operative had finished transmission, Washburn had written a second missive that said: 'Please inform I** that I hope to return to New York tomorrow, and will call in at the cave.' He signed it 'GW' and addressed it to Herr Charlie Pfaff at 647 Broadway. He folded it round bills to the value of twice the advertised transmission fee and winked as he slid it over the counter.

After watching the wires transmitted, the reporter ordered beans and scrambled eggs at a nearby café. Before he finished eating, steam engulfed the depot, and he gathered his things and dashed to the telegraph office to inquire after receipts from the *Tribune* or a permit to charter a train. The clerk merely shrugged, but the engineer on the locomotive gave a thumbs-up to his inquiry if the destination was Baltimore. Washburn threw his baggage, blanket and flasks through the door of a boxcar and heaved his body after them. Seconds later, the loco let out a screeching rasp and jolted fitfully out of Frederick.

Luck was running Washburn's way. Apart from being on track for the Rookery, anticipation of seeing Ida Godiva at Pfaff's Cave warmed his cockles. Writing was impossible aboard this juddering hobo's transport, so he continued to compose in his head as he had done all the previous night on horseback. He ranged over the to and fro of battle, the talents and shortcomings of McClellan's commanders and of McClellan himself. The more he reviewed the situation, the more he wondered if the Army of the Potomac was driving Lee, Jackson and company into the river, or if McClellan was waiting to see if the Rebels were slinking away or squaring up for another fight. The fate of the Union might be settled by the time he reached Baltimore. But Washburn the Bohemian doubted it.

The train ambled through countryside for hours, stopping to take on water or set down a box or collect barrels and bulging sacks. It rumbled into Baltimore ten minutes before the evening flyer to New York was due to depart. A ragged, dusty figure leaped from his boxcar and scrambled aboard the crowded express. All seats were taken, and so he propped himself up on a partition beneath a dim oil lamp at the end of a car and scribbled all through the night. He relived Antietam in a trance, his pencil wandering with the clickety-clack rhythm of the train and the emotive events that he was bent on bringing to life.

Sheet number one began:

A fierce and desperate battle between 200,000 men has raged by Antietam Creek since daylight, yet night closes on an uncertain field. It is the greatest fight since Waterloo – all over the field contested with obstinacy equal even to Waterloo. If not wholly a victory tonight, I believe it is the prelude to a victory tomorrow. But what can be foretold of the future of a fight which from five in the morning till seven at night the best troops of the continent have fought without decisive result?

He described the hellish struggle of the cornfields: 'Wondrous of bodies amid trampled stalks of regiments decimated by Hood's Texans … Across the road powder-blackened survivors of Greene's division of Mansfield's corps held ground round a riddled clapboard church … General Mansfield dead, two corps disorganized and two thousand of Sedgwick's men went down attempting to support them.'

The train steamed through the night, occasionally groaning to a halt at dingy stops. Washburn registered Wilmington, Philadelphia and Trenton as his sheaf of sheets grew thicker:

In ten minutes the fortune of the day changed … It was the Rebels now who were advancing … General Hooker sent in his nearest brigade to meet them, but it made no mark …

He described terrible slaughter in the farm lane known as the Sunken Road, and how General Burnside dallied fatally before crossing the triple-arched stone bridge when he might have delivered a decisive victory. He set in context the fight for control of South Mountain's passes and the surrender of the Union's armory at Harper's Ferry.

When Washburn disembarked at Jersey City in the pale light of morning, his pencil had written thousands of words describing the battle, analyzing tactics and speculating on the result of the bloodiest encounter of the war. Ever since Fort Sumter was attacked in what seemed eons ago, the Union's generals had lacked military success, despite their superior numbers and equipment. But in Washburn's opinion, Antietam would bring some cheer to President Lincoln in his hour of need. Whether it would be enough to spur him to unleash his emancipation declaration was a question awaiting an answer. Washburn didn't have the answer, and it was not a subject for speculation in the *Tribune*. Not yet.

He walked quickly to the Cortland Street boat for Manhattan, hunched on a seat and forced his sunken eyes to trawl through his masterpiece. On the cross-town omnibus he re-ordered the pages to his satisfaction before alighting at 152 Nassau Street, where he dragged his feet to the third floor to face the familiar command that gained entrance to the Rookery: EDITORIAL ROOMS OF THE TRIBUNE. RING THE BELL.

Doesticks Thomson admitted him, suppressing a gaping yawn as he grasped the elbow of the grubby traveler. The Rookery was eerily deserted at six o'clock in the morning save for half a dozen compositors in the far corner who jumped up and greeted the haggard and grubby correspondent with a cheer. Sydney Gay rushed from his room and broke into a broad grin as he welcomed his triumphant Bohemian.

'Well, you made it, Mr Washburn. The Washington office cabled that you were coming. I hope the journey has been worth your while.'

Washburn reached into his satchel and produced his wedge of numbered sheets. Doesticks dealt out slices to the comps, remarking that Washburn's text was scrawled in the least readable hand ever presented to the composing room for deciphering in tremulous haste.

'Did my telegram from Frederick get through yesterday morning?' asked Washburn.

'Eventually, yes,' Gay replied. 'It was diverted to the war department. They eventually alerted Wilkeson, who sat in their office while a copy was written out for him. You did well to hint at what was to come without giving much away.'

'The military do what suits them regardless,' Washburn said. He sank into the nearest chair, suddenly dog tired, hardly able to stand.

'Come, you'll be needing ablutions and rest. But we'll have to keep you here until the comps are satisfied that they can understand everything. You can use my washroom to freshen up, and Doesticks here will send out to Pfaff's for Charlie's finest Bavarian breakfast. We've arranged a room at the Coleman on Broadway, where you can sleep for as many days as you like, all found, and we'll get some new garb in for you. We'll send you off a true Bohemian, clutching a copy of the morning's special edition containing your pearls of prose! Meantime, there's coffee coming.'

With that, Washburn dumped his things on a desk and prepared to visit the washroom.

'One other thing,' Doesticks said. 'A letter was handed in for you yesterday, from Charlie Pfaff.'

Washburn broke the seal and unfolded the sheet.

'Call on Herr Pfaff, for he will know where is your angel,' it said.

12

A Banquet for Two

Later that morning, a gentle blow from what turned out to be a folded newspaper woke Washburn. He slowly raised his drowsy head, and the scales of slumber gradually fell away to transform the shadow standing over him into the managing editor. Eventually Washburn sat up and focused on Gay. 'You're released from further duties,' said the shadow, 'at least for today!' The reporter tried to form words, but nothing came out.

'Here's the first copy of your special to roll off the press, still warm from the Hoe. You've done a magnificent job, Washburn. The *Tribune* seems way ahead of the pack in intelligence from Antietam, thanks to your truly Bohemian enterprise. Rooms and hot tub await at the Coleman house, above Pfaff's cave, only a block from here. You'll no doubt welcome a new wardrobe after your escapades, and Doesticks has volunteered to attend to your needs. Settle at Coleman's while he acquires garb suitable for a *Tribune* Bohemian. If you feel like meeting him for sustenance later, he'll give you all the news.'

Washburn stirred, rose, pushed aside the remains of Pfaff's breakfast, pocketed his note from Ida, gathered up his haversack, hoisted his saddlebag onto the desk, picked up the paper, held it out at arm's length and read aloud from the heading on the six-column special:

New York Tribune Special Edition

The Battle of Antietam
Army of the Potomac in Greatest Fight Since Waterloo

By Our Own Correspondent
Battlefield of Sharpsburg
Wednesday Evening, September 17, 1862

'I'm honored, sir,' he said, looking his editor in the eye while he rolled up the special, tucked it under his arm and turned toward the door. 'Please tell Doesticks that I'll see him at the Cave around two o'clock once I've cleaned up.'

'Call back here when you've recovered, and bring an account of your expenses,' Gay said.

The special correspondent walked directly to the Coleman and collapsed on the bed as soon as he was shown to his rooms, still wearing the battle-torn garments that he had inhabited for weeks. He could detect an aura about his person that encouraged others to keep their distance. He was woken two hours later by a delivery of new clothes courtesy of the *Tribune* – a linen shirt with upstanding collar, a broad-lapelled vest and a thigh-length sack coat, wide floppy necktie and trousers. He ran the hot faucet and sank into the tub, scrubbed himself down – ah, bliss! – and found that his new attire, more Bohemian than formal, fitted his frame well enough. The card inside the wrapping advertised 'Brooks Brothers on Cherry and Catherine, serving all men's tailoring needs, including ready-made garments'. He checked his new look again in the glass, donned the brown derby from the brothers' emporium at a jaunty angle, and hastened along Broadway to

Pfaff's, where Doesticks was waiting.

At three o'clock they were sitting in Charlie's cave sipping German beer and exchanging pleasantries about the Coleman House Hotel and the products of Brown Brothers. Ida's intimate message was warm in Washburn's pocket, inviting him to call at the Albemarle on Madison Square after six, 'where a banquet and all angelic comforts await him', signed 'I'. It was hard to concentrate on his colleague's account of the route by which the electric telegraph had conveyed his message to New York.

'When it arrived in Baltimore the agent at American Telegraph pounced on it and relayed it to the war department, so by noon that day it was in Lincoln's hands. It was the first intelligence to reach the president since McClellan's "we are in the midst of the most terrible battle of the war" message sent the previous afternoon. Anyhow, Hill and Wilkeson got wind that your report was at the war department, and at one-thirty a clerk there began to copy it page by page while Wilkeson stood over him. He persuaded Sanford, who's president of the telegraph company, to order his Baltimore operator to send it on to New York, but Baltimore did not comply. At about half past ten Hill sent a message to Gay saying that he had visited the telegraph office a second time and was assured that, to that hour, no dispatch from the battle had come over the wires from any other source.'

Doesticks paused to sip his beer.

'Gay's dancing round the Rookery because you've beaten the *Herald* and the *Times* out of sight. He acknowledges that your *Tribune* team are devoted to their work, while the *Herald* has so many men in the field that they forget to get the news out. And he thinks the *Times* lacks organization. He's also relieved that Coffin's *Journal* is in Boston, and not competing on the streets of New York. He told me to tell you that your story is more than worthy of Crimea Bill. He called it a masterpiece, a thunderous beat, a restrained graphical account with conviction, explaining the battle plan over the whole field. He said it identifies that the army's poor co-ordination is leading to a stalemate. You're the only authority in town tonight, for sure.'

Washburn, trying his best to absorb what Doesticks was saying, signaled for more beer, more sticks and more *pfannekuchen*.

'Well, that's all very flattering,' he said. 'I must say that several times I asked myself what I thought I was doing during the last three nights or however long it's been, so it's gratifying to hear that it was worth it.'

'I should tell you,' Doesticks went on, 'that Gay was riled to receive seven pages from Paige complaining that you spent more time carrying messages for the army than looking to the *Tribune*'s interests. He accuses you of considering him a coward for not going under fire when he saw nothing to be gained by it. On the other hand ...' and he raised a hand – 'let me finish ... Richardson wrote to Gay to beg him to caution you to be more prudent, but he was full of admiration nevertheless, saying that it is wonderful that you came out of battle with your life. Evans, too, has sent Gay a character reference. And Gay said you have proved Wilkeson's theory that successful battle reporting lays in being so closely observant as to be in danger of being killed.'

'I'm not sure about that, but I guess tempers got a little ragged by the end of the day,' Washburn said. 'Paige lacks insight on the field, whereas Al Richardson knows instinctively where to be and what to do. Evans too.'

'Anyways, it's all been worth it, all right,' Doesticks said. 'For one thing, it underlines the paper's skepticism over the leadership qualities of Young Napoleon. Old Horace Greeley should be tripping the light fantastic. For another, the battle and its account may persuade Lincoln to free the slaves. If Lee is beat, France and Britain's support for the Rebel government will very likely wilt. There's tremendous thirst for news of Sharpsburg and Antietam because so much hangs on the result. Inquiries about syndication rates were flying in to the Rookery by noon, and when I left there were orders on the table from the *New York Times*, the London *Times*, the Philly *Inquirer* and *Harper's*. Your story is going to sweep the world, and it'll pay your wages, and mine besides. By the way, I have permission to charge this to Greeley's coffers.'

Their conversation drifted to other matters as they picked at *pfannekuchen* and quaffed Pfaff's lager. Presently, Bohemians began to drift down the steps to the cave, and Washburn decided it was time he made his excuses.

'I haven't the energy to roister here this evening. Maybe tomorrow, so if you don't mind I'll go back to the hotel and get some more beauty sleep,' he said, thinking of the Albemarle. 'And by the way, many thanks again for my new outfit. I think I'll visit the Brooks emporium and re-stock my wardrobe.'

'Believe Abe Lincoln is a customer,' Doesticks said, signaling to the waitress to settle for the fare. 'You deserve plenty of rest. See you at the Rookery in a day or two, or here later, though perhaps you have another engagement. I did hear that the Godiva's in town.' An inquiring smile flickered over his face.

Washburn flashed Doesticks a look as he stood up and made haste. Once in the street he hailed a cab and directed the driver downtown to Cherry and Catherine, where he bought himself a 'ditto' suit of coat, vest and trousers in matching cloth. It was the latest item in the Brothers' style repertoire, straight off the rail and 'made to the perfect fit' according to the obsequious attendant.

Washburn wore his new ditto suit and derby when he departed the Coleman to walk to the Albemarle. The bullet that struck his flask was in his pocket, wrapped in a sheet from his notebook and addressed to his guardian angel. A copy of the *Tribune* special was under his arm. He took a detour off Broadway to kill time, wondering at the assignation that he has gotten himself into. Reality struck with force. He didn't really know anything about Ida. An hour in the crowded cave a year ago had made a powerful impression and kept him going during the worse times in the field, but in a few minutes he would face a woman with whom he had no common ground save a brush on the nape of his neck. Perhaps they would have nothing to say to one another. He mustn't play the battlefield hero or arrogant scribe. But he also reminded himself that she needn't have replied to his suggestive letter, nor could she be short of suitors, so Cupid's dart must have struck her as it did him.

As he swung back into Broadway he passed the Canterbury, a concert saloon with a reputation for revealing outfits, blue acts and lecherous magicians. Forrester Williams once told him 'from a usually unreliable source' that Ida performed there. When the Albemarle came into sight, he wondered how difficult it might be to discover her past. Perhaps best not to delve.

The opulent surroundings of the hotel excited him. It stood at the junction of Broadway and Fifth Avenue opposite Madison Square, a commanding position in the uptown hotchpotch of theaters, saloons, vaudeville haunts, fancy restaurants and cheap hasheries, places of worship and houses of ill repute, halls, clubs and stores. At this hour actors and musicians thronged the sidewalks on their way to work, and street-walkers plied for business.

Washburn admired Ida's choice of rendezvous. The Albemarle's five floors of brick and white marble opened to a lofty lobby and grand reception. Every facet was luxurious. A glimpse of the dining rooms revealed elaborate frescoes and upholstery. Wide corridors led to spacious staircases augmented by the latest in the architect's lexicon, an elevator that conveyed guests to the upper floors. Washburn sidled into the saloon and the reading room and was flattered to see several guests engrossed in copies of the special supplement that was tucked under his arm.

He presented his *carte de visite* at the desk and asked confidently for Miss Ida, hoping that she went by that name, for he didn't have any other. 'Take a seat, sir,' said the clerk, snapping his fingers and passing the card to a bell boy who receded up the stairway two steps at a time. Washburn took a deep breath and sat on a couch.

Presently the boy returned and showed him into the elevator, a wondrous contraption that was moved up and down by a vertical screw encased in a cylinder that passed through the center of the car and was connected to a steam engine in the basement. At the fifth floor the boy tapped on the door of suite 5-1, and a uniformed maid ushered Washburn into a mahogany-paneled reception room where a table was set for two. A bottle of champagne rested in an ice bucket, and a sideboard displayed brandy, rum, whiskey and an open box of cigarettes. A slight waft of tobacco hung in the room. The nightrider pinched himself. Twenty-four hours ago he could not have imaged such fairyland luxury that surrounded him now.

The maid interrupted his reverie. 'Miss Ida begs forbearance for a few minutes. She asks if you would like a hot tub after your ride from Washington? Is there something you require?'

'Nothing save Miss Ida's presence, thank you. Please apologize for my late arrival. I overslept when I reached New York, first time I'd seen a proper bed in weeks, so I'm a little out of sorts ...'

'Not a trouble, sir. Miss Ida's going to order for eight o'clock.'

Just then Ida's voice called out 'Rosa', and the maid disappeared through double doors. Washburn could just catch Ida's words: 'We'll go for the royal dishes as the chef here is French and reputed to be the best in New York. So, two Coburg soups, two fillets of beef *a la Prince Albert,* rare, and two Alexander tortes, whoever Alexander is. And a bottle of the sommelier's best French claret. Offer our guest champagne or his preferred liquor and let him see our choices on your way out, for I don't wish to present him with something he doesn't eat or drink. Here at eight o'clock, not before. And apologize to Mr Washburn for keeping him waiting.'

The wonderful prerogative of a woman and a hostess. Washburn glanced over the order, signaled approval and accepted champagne. Rosa performed a little curtsey on her way to the kitchen, and Washburn noted her sparkling eyes and dapper movements like a thespian. He parted the drapes at the window and surveyed the human tide milling around the square below. Then he settled on a couch and placed his gift together with the special edition of the *Tribune* on a footstool.

Wall-mounted gas lamps held evening shadows at bay. An eerie silence wrapped itself around humming bursts of *Yankee Doodle Dandy* from the inner suite. He half closed his eyes and bade himself to sit still.

After what seemed like an age the doors opened and an electrical charge filled the room. A stunning vision advanced before him, a beauty far superior to the image he carried from Pfaff's Cave on his first fateful visit to the Rookery. Azure eyes set in porcelain skin met his gaze. Her lips were a subtle red. Honey blonde ringlets fell to her shoulders. Sparkling drop earrings glistered, and a glittering choker adorned her throat. A silk gown in shimmering cerise was secured by a silver clasp and flowed through the valley of her chest to a hemline inches short of her feet. The silky folds occasionally gave glimpse of shapely legs rising from delicate feet supported by black boots, the height of which Washburn had only seen on high kickers in low saloons.

Washburn opened his mouth to speak, but no words emerged. Ida, though, found her soft voice. 'So the conquering hero comes to claim his angel, and perhaps to dine in her rooms.' Her eyes drank him in. 'And she has a terrible thirst, so please pour the fizz, kind sir. Dinner's not until eight, so we have time to get acquainted.' A long muscle-toned calf and thigh emerged from folds of silk.

Washburn poured a flute and made to give it to her as she tugged the clasp at her neck and sent the gown cascading to the floor. She stepped out of it and stood before him, clad but in boots and sparkling jewels. She entwined her drinking arm through his and took a swift draft, turned and led him toward the flickering candlelight of heaven's antechamber.

Thus George Washburn embarked on his third ride in forty-eight hours, this time in the arms of his Bohemian princess.

13

War and Peace

Friday, 14 April 1865, Ford's Theater, Washington
George Washburn's Saturday night with Ida lasted until Monday morning. The lovers' exploration in the Albemarle's four-poster was interrupted only by a visit to the Delmonico brothers' much-vaunted Citadel restaurant on South William Street, where they feasted on steak, the house specialty, washed down by fine French claret. Stardust enveloped Ida from the moment they darkened Delmonico's door. She acted oblivious of diners feasting on the sight of her, while Washburn's skin was burning. Flatteringly, the diners' attention focused on her, but she only had eyes for him.

Once at the table, he found courage enough to ask after her upbringing. She never knew her parents, and was raised in New Orleans by a couple of vaudeville performers who recognized her talent for singing and dancing. They shepherded their child star onto the boards of the opera house and put her to work with a song-and-dance routine aboard Mississippi paddle steamers. She was grateful for the way they had treated her but was less forthcoming about her life between child prodigy and bareback stardom. Washburn didn't press it.

On Monday morning the lovers resolved to meet in Pfaff's that evening after Washburn had attended on his editors and Ida had kept her appointment with the showman Phineas T Barnum who, said the invitation, had a proposition to put to her.

Part of Washburn wished to avoid the Rookery for as long as possible, but he was impatient to learn what Gay would do with him next. Besides, he had not been paid for a month. Meager reporters' wages of $15 to $35 a week compared with compositors' $50 necessitated exaggerated claims for expenses, much to the annoyance of the keepers of newspaper counting houses, including Sam Sinclair, the *Tribune's* penny-pinching business manager. In Pfaff's on the previous Saturday, Doesticks had tutored Washburn on the art of claiming expenses, and reminded him that his Antietam adventure deserved a leg up. 'Homer the artist gets sixty bucks for a double page spread in *Harper's*,' he said, 'and he probably carries a library of cloud formations ready for embellishment, so you ought to hang in for $50, maybe more. Now is your chance, my son. When it comes to expenses, essential equipment has become marvelously elaborate, and servants are indispensable. Take a leaf out of Crimea Bill's inventory for venturing into the unknown!'

On his way to the Rookery, Washburn reflected that inflating expenses was difficult when shadowing an army in the wilderness with no opportunity to run up bills at the likes of Delmonico's. He had, however, compiled an impressive docket.

As he walked down Broadway, the twin tails of a long, white coat flying out behind a swaying figure caught his eye. A tall floppy hat crowned the phenomenon whose trouser bottoms were bunched into coarse, muddy boots. Such garb could only encase Horace Greeley, his paymaster and editor-in-chief. Washburn followed at a distance until Greeley dived into Windust's restaurant, a few doors short of the *Tribune* building.

Washburn climbed the stairs to the third floor in twos, straight to Gay's office where he was bidden to take a seat. 'I must tell you that Greeley passes on his good wishes and congratulations for performing a marvelous job for the paper and the Union. But he's due here any minute, so he can tell you himself. We've syndicated to more than a hundred papers so far, so your words girdle the globe. My proposal – and Mr G agrees – is for you to go back to the army as soon as possible and stay close to McClellan. Lincoln is said to be furious that Lee is not drowned in the Potomac. Wilkeson has it that the president is contemplating a visit to the general, which can only mean one of two things: a boot up his nether parts or dismissal. Lincoln is said to be in ecstasy about your report, by the way. He's worrying about the congressional elections and putting an end to slavery, if you ask me.'

'I was hoping to visit my old folks upstate in Troy where my father is now the pastor, but perhaps that can wait. I would surely like to see McClellan's story through. But I would also point out that I'm on a very low remuneration …'

'What are we paying you? Twenty bucks? You haven't had a raise since joining? How does forty sound?'

'Fifty sounds better, Mr Gay. And I'm owed expenses for the Antietam adventure.'

'We can shake on fifty dollars a week. Let me sign those,' and Gay glanced quickly through the piece of paper that Washburn slid across the desk:

- Salary 6 weeks owing until 21 Sept '62 at $20 = $120
- 1 ream paper, stamps and stamped envelopes $5.75
- Willard's Hotel 28 nights retainer @ $5 = $140
- To New York via Frederick and Baltimore, RR expenses and gratuities $20
- Field mattress, pillow and blanket $13
- Saddle, bridle, halter, saddle-blanket $28
- Forage, stabling etc. $12 (8 per month to quartermaster)

Gay made a pencil mark at each item. When he reached 'Horse and saddle, bridle, halter, saddle-blanket,' he asked, 'Didn't Mr Hill find you a horse?'

'Found, yes, but it was paid from my own pocket. He was due at the bank and I had to get along.'

'Fine,' Gay said, and signed at the bottom. 'Take this to Mr Sinclair, and watch him scowl. Can't bare parting with dollar bills, can Mr Sinclair.'

'It'll be a pleasure,' Washburn said. 'I'll head out for Washington and McClellan's camp on the morrow.'

A few minutes later, making for the door with a wedge of bills in his pocket, he was caught in a flurry as Greeley entered, brushing aside hopeful petitioners. Greeley grasped Washburn's hand warmly. 'Keep up the good work,' he said, his sparkling blue eyes penetrating the reporter. 'I have it on good authority that you have fired up President Lincoln.'

Washburn tripped down the staircase into the rest of his stay in New York. The prospect before him was an evening with Bohemians at Pfaff's followed by a third night of passion.

There was lively company at Pfaff's, including several Bohemian artists visiting New York to deliver their interpretations of Antietam. In response to goading from the King, Henri Lovie embellished the sacrifice he had made on behalf of *Leslie's Weekly*. 'I am deranged about the stomach, ragged, unkempt and unshorn, and need the co-joined skill and services of the apothecary, the tailor and the barber.'

While the King tut-tutted, Washburn sympathized, having visited the barber, the apothecary and Brown brother's clothing store earlier in the day.

'Among the least of my sorrows are riding fifteen miles a day through mud and underbrush and then working until midnight by the dim light of a tallow dip,' Lovie continued. His diatribe aroused a figure resting his sunburned head on spread-eagled arms.

'You think you artistes have it bad,' said the aroused. 'The only companion we Bohemian scribes enjoy while roaming the wastes of the Old Dominion under a mid-summer brass sky heated to a frazzle by a pitiless sun, as I have done, is danger without the soldier's glory. Grit is in the air you breathe. Fatigue and sleeplessness are your constant companions as you are boiled, panted and thirsted.'

Washburn recognized the speaker as Charles Page of the *Tribune*, having seen him once before in the Rookery. As Page opened his mouth to continue, a strapping blue-eyed man who introduced himself as Alfred Waud of *Harper's* raised his arms to encourage the company to contribute their hyperboles of life on the battlefield.

Page recited onwards into the sunset. 'Ride for fifteen hours, ride for fifty miles until you halt to eat and drink long after dark, longing for a cake of soap. You squat like a toad before a campfire and with a stubby pencil in hand and battling smoke from the fire and ashes on your paper, begin to compose. Your brain's fuzzed ...'

Waud, a stalwart being with a fair beard, jack-booted, gauntleted, armed and crowned with a slouch hat, was on his feet again. He broke into a jeer and, egged on by Clapp, sang scraps of marching songs in an attempt to drown Page out.

'... you're in pain and torment, and when you are done, for hell's sake don't read it over, or you will throw it into the fire. At dawn you awake to find your horse and saddlebags gone. The worst thing is to come upon your piece in print and see how your dispatches have been botched by illiterate tampering so-called editors who think they know more about your subject than you do, and think they possess the liberty to mess up your words.'

Rousing cheers.

Conversation eventually shifted from accusations of romanticizing the war leveled at artists to condemnation of penny paper hacks who wrote of 'unparalleled gallantry' of Union soldiers who 'fought like tigers' and made-up speeches beseeching boys to 'stand up for the Union and rally to the old flag!'

Spurred on, Page raised questions of meaning.

'Prey, if I write down my *Tribune* colleague Washburn's words verbatim, I am accurate, but not necessarily faithful to what he is saying,' he announced to the company round the table. 'For example, if I quote Washburn here as saying that the King of Bohemia should be hanged, drawn and quartered, how is the reader to know whether Washburn speaks with irony or serious intent to topple the monarch?' Page genuflected toward King Clapp. 'The scribe must somehow transfer the meaning, the *sound,* the *intonation* of Washburn's speech on to paper. It's more important to get that across than to record it verbatim. Not the easiest of skills. Especially as a sentence commands more authority once it is set in type.'

The banter that followed encompassed the merits or otherwise of objectivity, subjectivity and Clapp's prospects of staying alive before Page steered it back to cheap papers and their journalism.

'The penny papers habitually represent a body of troops as eager for the fray, burning to be led against the foe or spoiling for a fight. Such writers know nothing of armies and have probably never been near a battle. Soldiers mock them, for soldiers do not hold amorous inclinations toward bullets.'

'Nor do horses, creatures for whom nobody gives a thought,' Washburn said. 'I've as much respect for them as for men under fire. They are truly remarkable. I was once accompanying General Pope when he exposed us to sudden enemy fire. There was nothing we riders could do but sit in the saddle while the horses galloped over unknown country, terrain stiff with fences and brooks, at full speed without making a single mistake. I never before gave a thought to the intelligence of that animal. Nobody came to grief; nor, which seems wonderful, did anybody stop a bullet. But a good many remarks found their mark on General Pope!'

Page stood and invited the company to raise their glasses to Washburn, 'the most syndicated writer in the history of the press', for the insight displayed in his Antietam dispatch. Even the King obliged, despite his irritation at all things *Tribunal*, Greeley-esque or Bostonian.

Washburn took his leave of Pfaff's when Ida, who some time back had slipped into her customary seat at the Bohemian royal family's end of the table, drained her glass, blew an expert smoke ring, stubbed out her cigarette and sent her lover a come-hither wink. Next morning he took a train to Washington, having promised to keep her informed of his whereabouts, and she of hers.

Washburn put up at Willard's for a couple of nights to be fed the latest on the friction between the president and his field commander. When he arrived at the *Tribune*'s paper-strewn, inky microcosm of the Rookery, Hill poured a large glass of whiskey.

'Welcome back to Washington,' he said, thrusting the glass into Washburn's hand and grasping the other. 'Ever since your special appeared, we *Tribune* men have merely to lean on the White House door to gain admittance. Lincoln's been keen to share his thoughts.'

For several hours Washburn was presented with a comprehensive account of moods in the center of government. 'President Lincoln is set on his emancipation proclamation and itching to turn the stalemate of Antietam into victory,' Hill said. 'If the Army of Potomac pursued Lee now, Lincoln argues, it would put itself between the Confederate forces and Richmond and be advantageously positioned for a fight to the finish. But, you guessed it, McClellan hasn't lifted a finger, while Lee's army is re-equipping a few miles west of Harper's Ferry.'

He poured more whiskey.

'Lincoln instructed Halleck to order McClellan to cross the Potomac and give battle. McClellan declared that he could not move until his supply wagons were full. This triggered Halleck's exasperated retort that "it requires the lever of Archimedes to move this inert mass". He wrote to Lincoln that he was sick, tired and disgusted with McClellan's inactivity. "There is an immobility here that exceeds all that any man can conceive of", was how he put it,' Hill said with a chuckle.

With Lincoln's proclamation out of the bag, debate raged from all sides over its likely effect once it arrived in the public domain. While Greeley's *Tribune* urged the president on, supporters and detractors took up pens. Hill indicated a pile of clippings on his desk and pulled a few out at random. The New York Democratic platform denounced the proposal as 'butchery of women and children in scenes of lust and rapine, and of arson and murder'. A Republican paper opined that 'a large majority can see no reason why they should be shot for the benefit of niggers and abolitionists'. Hill also said that there was much argument over putting blacks in the army.

'The most important thing I found out,' Hill said, 'was that

Lincoln informed his cabinet that he had made a covenant with God that if the army drove the enemy from Maryland he would issue his proclamation. It would say that unless Confederate states returned to the Union by first of January next, their slaves shall be set free. "Free then, henceforward, and forever" is how he put it. Critics allege that this might drive border states into the arms of the South and hand Democrats a club with which to beat the administration in the congressional elections. As a lawyer you will appreciate that the proclamation refers only to states in rebellion on the first of January, thus appearing to liberate only those slaves beyond the Union's authority while retaining bondage for those within the government's reach. Where Lincoln has no power he will set the slaves free ...'

'... but where he exercises power he will consider them as slaves,' Washburn finished the sentence for him. 'Under the constitution the president has no power to act against slavery in areas loyal to the United States. So if the army wins the war it will become an army of liberation on the first day of January. The character of the war will change to one of subjugation. The old South will be destroyed and replaced by new propositions and ideas, dictated from the North.'

'But some doubt that the army will fight to free slaves, especially McClellan's divisions, because he has Democratic inclinations and does not support the proclamation,' Hill said.

'Yes, Mac made plain his opposition to freeing slaves as a war aim when Lincoln met him at Harrison's Landing way back in the summer. If I recall it right,' Washburn said. 'So if old Abe issues his proclamation, he'll go head to head with his obtuse general. In any case, his covenant with God as told to the cabinet commits McClellan to move.'

'But will the army fight for freedom, I ask myself?' said Hill. 'Not many soldiers are abolitionists, but a great many wish to destroy anything that gives the Rebels strength, including slavery. I heard Halleck say that we must conquer the Rebels or be conquered by them. He calculates that every slave withdrawn from the enemy is the equivalent of a white man put *hors de combat*.'

Washburn took a train to Frederick, the closest railhead to the army's camping grounds around Antietam Creek. Among his baggage was a notebook full of ifs and buts on three burning Union issues: freedom for slaves, relations with Britain and European powers and congressional elections due in the fall. He collected the horse and bridle he had hired by telegraph from the Frederick livery, and set out for Sharpsburg.

His route took him over the scene of the battle: territory shrouded in melancholy, devoid of birdsong and farmyard sounds. Scattered parties of medical orderlies wore face mufflers as they piled bodies and dismembered parts of bodies into wagons. Here and there army engineers attempted to restore order from chaos by repairing fences, corduroying muddy fields with log roads, removing wrecked guns and uprooting *chevaux-de-frise*, the spiked logs planted for defense against marauding infantry.

The horse picked its dexterous way over lost items from knapsacks and haversacks. Canteens, flasks, 'housewife' sowing kits lay in the mud, the detritus of the dead and wounded. Washburn spied Gardner the photographer on the horizon, his head inside his magic box to capture truthful images of horror for display at his Daguerreian gallery. The thought sent a shudder through Washburn, and his body was numb until he entered Sharpsburg and found a lodging house.

Next morning the reporter took a tour round streets festooned with Union flags. He passed a couple of makeshift saloons and several homes advertising hot meals, business enterprises set up by townsfolk whose peaceful daily lives had been upended by two enormous belligerent armies. Washburn's landlady had questioned his officer status when he first knocked on her door with its notice announcing 'ROOMS'. She explained that General McClellan had banished all but ranking officers from within the bounds of the little town. Many townsfolk who, like farmers in the surrounding country, had been evacuated from the battle area were now reclaiming their properties and seeking ways of profiting by hundreds of bored officers living under canvas among the farmsteads. He learned later that an abandoned building on the outskirts of the town had been converted into a house of ill repute, serviced by painted Jezebels from Washington.

Once Sharpsburg's streets and facilities were mapped in his mind, Washburn headed out to McClellan's HQ to look for Strother. The general's senior aide greeted him with a smile, saying that his Antietam report had been read widely and appreciated widely in army circles. 'I don't know if Mac has read it. If he has, he hasn't said anything within earshot.'

Later they rode into Sharpsburg and stopped at a saloon to compare notes on McClellan's failure to pursue Lee across the Potomac. Washburn traded his information about the proclamation for the latest news on the standoff between McClellan and the war department. Had McClellan shown any reaction to the *Tribune*'s journalism since firing ceased? he inquired, to which Strother answered no. 'But the both of us must be careful,' Strother said. 'If he gets the idea that I, his trusted servant, am feeding criticism of him to the press, I'll be heading for a court martial, and if he gets the idea that your dispatches are negative, you and your paper will be heading for censorship, or even banishment.'

'Agreed,' Washburn answered. 'I must give space to his ideas and opinions, make him feel that the *Tribune* is, if not on his side, not against him.'

They clinked glasses and agreed to meet to compare notes discreetly on a daily basis.

The standoff, fueled by rumors of the proclamation, ran into October. On one occasion Lincoln visited McClellan's headquarters unannounced and asked the general if he was not over-cautious to assume that he couldn't do what the enemy was constantly doing? McClellan asserted that his men needed new shoes and full stomachs before they could be expected to march twenty miles a day. While Lincoln became more and more conscious of time passing, Strother observed that McClellan was detaching himself, murmuring to his officers that Commander-in-Chief Halleck should be answerable to him, and Secretary for War Stanton should be removed. He was also heard to say that the proclamation was infamous, and he could not fight for such an accursed doctrine as servile insurrection.

'I think he thinks he is superior to Lincoln, let alone Halleck,' Strother remarked to Washburn.

On another occasion Strother let slip that Lincoln cashiered an officer for spreading rumor of a conspiracy that had both armies staying in the field at Antietam until exhausted, when a compromise would be made, and slavery saved.

McClellan's next justification for staying put was that many of his horses were broken down, eliciting another furious riposte from Lincoln: 'Will you pardon me for asking what the horses of your army have done since the battle of Antietam that fatigues anything?'

Nothing fatigued McClellan's horses like Jeb Stuart's adventure as commander of the Rebel cavalry. Stuart cocked a snoop at the Army of the Potomac in the second week of October by leading his men right round its encampment and returning to Virginia after two days with 12,000 captive horses at the cost of two human casualties.

Washburn and Strother noted that for all his obfuscation, McClellan was careful to remain on the right side of the law. On 7 October he issued a general order reminding officers of the necessity for military subordination to civil authority. The remedy for political errors is at the polls, he reiterated, no doubt with his own polling prospects in mind.

One quiet afternoon, the reporter and the aide turned their thoughts to foreign relations. Washburn raised the hypocrisy of the British. 'First they enrich themselves with their cruel slave trade, then they abolish the trade and enforce its abolition with their navy. Then they abolish slavery on their Caribbean islands, and now they support slavery in the South to grow the cotton that they need to feed Lancashire's garment mills. If they threw in their lot with the Rebels, the blockade of the South would be broken and Lincoln would have to go to war with the Royal Navy, which would spell disaster for the Union.'

'There's another factor which I heard about only the other day,' Strother said. 'The army is running short of saltpeter.'

'Saltpeter?'

'It's an essential ingredient of gunpowder, and it is found in India. Only in India.'

'So the Royal Navy controls the saltpeter trade.'

'They must be burning the oil late at the war department.'

'Not only that,' Washburn said. 'My friends in Washington have wind of a diplomatic dispute that threatens to bring Britain into the war. Apparently the Confeds dispatched plenipotentiaries to Britain and France last month by running the blockade out of Charleston and putting them aboard a British merchantman, the *Trent*, I think that's her name, in Havana. But when the *Trent* departed Cuba, the *USS Jacinto* grasped the bull by the horns, so to speak, and took the agents into custody while allowing the ship to proceed. The captain of *Jacinto*, a maverick by the name of Wilkes, acted without orders and in breach of international law. He should have arrested the British ship and impounded it in the prize court. The Washington rumor mill says that the British press is clamoring for war, and Palmerston's government has set an embargo on trade with us. It's also rumored that they have sent more vessels to the western Atlantic, more troops to Canada and set an ultimatum for the release of the agents. And sure as hell is hot, the saltpeter factor must play into their hands.'

'There's another bone of contention with Britain,' Washburn continued. 'The British take a conveniently liberal interpretation of neutrality when it comes to shipbuilding. Thomas Dudley, the Union consul in Liverpool, claims he has evidence that a Southern agent ordered two steam-sail cruisers from a Liverpool shipyard last summer. As you know, neutrality forbids supply of arms and armament to belligerents. But this man Bulloch's ships slipped through the legal net due to bureaucratic nonsense, legal pettifoggery and the Liverpool customs collector's sympathies with the Rebels. Both ships avoided detention by embarking for trials on the Mersey River. In the case of the *Alabama*, she set sail two months ago and carried on cruising to the Azores, where she's been fitted out with armor and guns made in Britain and shipped out by tender. I wager that the excursion came as a surprise to the guests and the brass band who were on board for her trials! I guess they were dropped off as they passed out of the River Mersey! Anyway, if I was the navy department I'd be preparing a case for compensation from Her Majesty's Government.'

The Army of the Potomac began to cross into Virginia on 26 October, five weeks after the fight at Antietam. Progress was so slow that Lee could deploy his men in the way of Richmond, while Jackson blocked the Shenandoah Valley. Washburn's first letter to the *Tribune* from Virginian soil said that any chance of an immediate military end to the war had been lost, and the blame lay squarely at the feet of the Young Napoleon.

On 7 November Lincoln's patience snapped. He sacked McClellan and appointed Ambrose Burnside commander of the Army of the Potomac. McClellan's farewell message appealed to his troops to stand by Burnside. Burnside himself thought he was unworthy to take command, but on 15 November he marched his army south to Falmouth, a small Virginia town halfway between Washington and Richmond. Falmouth faced Fredericksburg, on the south bank of the Rappahannock River. On 11 December Washburn witnessed Burnside's pontoniers laying their floating bridge over the water, and after a fierce engagement between snipers and artillery, Union soldiers sacked Fredericksburg, but failed to breach Richmond's defenses. Once again, Washburn wrote, poor command of good troops was thwarted by effective Confederate generalship. As the first day of January approached, the day when Lincoln intended to proclaim emancipation, the president was no nearer to total victory.

Washburn sent his story on its way with relief. He had lacked energy for the past few days, and his brow became feverish. He soon developed a headache and was struck by abdominal pain. From what he knew of diseases that haunted armies, his symptoms pointed to typhoid fever, and his fear was confirmed by a conversation with a surgeon at the field ambulance station.

'We don't know its cause or its cure,' said the sawbones. 'Get yourself to a sanitorium in Washington and keep to yourself until you feel better is the best advice I can give you.'

Thus Washburn was absent for a month, isolated in a hospital on the fringe of the capital, with hardly the energy to put pen to paper. He scrawled notes to his elderly mother in Troy and Ida who was out west with Barnum's show. When he regained his strength, Gay directed him to join Adams Hill in Washington while Sam Wilkeson was away on a madcap exploit to report from Rebel Virginia under cover. Hill was to concentrate on politics and Washburn on military affairs. The latter's first reports covered Lincoln's public announcement of freedom for slaves in Confederate states from 1 January, and Burnside's replacement by Joe Hooker as commander of the Army of the Potomac.

Washburn quickly settled into the round of lobbying and rumormongering in the capital, and although missing Ida, her absence added frisson to their rare meetings. Whereas Hill much preferred life in Washington to the environs of the Rookery, Washburn found reasons to visit Manhattan, especially when Ida was in residence. One such tryst coincided with the government's introduction of conscription for twenty to forty-five-year-olds, a measure that included an exemption clause on receipt of a $300 fee. Critics saw this as unfair to working men who could not afford to buy exemption. Greeley welcomed the measure in his editorial as a device to relieve the army of bad fighters and contribute much-needed funds to the treasury.

The question of conscription exploded on the streets of New York when laborers rampaged through the city burning and looting, strung black men from lampposts and clubbed down abolitionists. Greeley's Rookery was a target, and when rioters approached, his friends whisked the editor-in-chief away to an early dinner in another part of town. Windows were shattered, furniture wrecked, gas lamps twisted from the wall and floors scorched by attempts to fire the building. All but three of the 150 journalists and printers in the building escaped via the roof. Washburn was one of the three, brandishing his pistol at the entrance to the editorial floor in an engagement far more frightening than guarding Wendell Phillips in Boston years ago. He was mighty relieved when the police arrived to move the rioters on. The next day's *Tribune* appeared on the streets as usual, its front page featuring an account by a special correspondent of assault on the Rookery.

The war raged on. Hooker lost a battle at Chancellorsville, Virginia, in May, but Ulysses Grant's army laid siege to Vicksburg and forced the Rebel stronghold on the Mississippi to surrender after holding out for six weeks. The mighty river fell to the Union.

Hooker's plan was to attack Richmond in June, but he was thwarted by Lee's unexpected departure from Fredericksburg into Pennsylvania via the Blue Ridge Mountains, intent on obtaining supplies and undermining civilian morale. Fighting Joe resigned his command and was replaced by George Meade, who engaged Lee at Gettysburg on 1 July. Lee was, as usual, outnumbered and compelled to retreat on the third day of battle, suffering 28,000 dead or wounded against the Meade's 23,000 casualties.

The *Tribune*'s scoop of the bloodbath at Gettysburg was delivered by A Homer Byington who, when a dozen miles from the battleground, noticed that a five-mile stretch of telegraph line along the train tracks had been cut down by Confederate cavalry. Leaving cover of the opening moves to others, Byington sought out the local telegraph operator, sent him to fetch battery and sounder and cut a deal with him for exclusive services. Byington then assembled a repair crew, commandeered spools of wire from a warehouse, rented a railroad handcar and spent a day re-stringing the line. At dusk on the second day of battle the *Tribune* received the first comprehensive report via Byington's line, while relays of *Herald* riders had to travel fifty miles to reach the nearest wire.

The gray army abandoned 7,000 casualties to be tended by volunteer doctors and nurses where they fell. The Union's victories at Gettysburg and Vicksburg signaled to both sides that the Rebels were tottering, and any hope harbored in Richmond of recognition by foreign governments faded. The victories once again raised Lincoln's hopes of bringing the war to a swift end, but once again the Army of the Potomac failed to chase Lee's forces back to Virginia. Meade did not catch up with Lee for twelve days, and when he crossed the river after further delay he encountered only the Rebel rear guard. Lincoln's acid comment to Hill was that Meade would be ready to fight a magnificent battle when there was no enemy to fight.

The slaughter at Gettysburg led to the dedication of a military cemetery where President Lincoln's opening address resounded round the world in print:

'Four score and seven years ago our fathers brought forth, on this continent, a new nation, conceived in Liberty, and dedicated to the proposition that all men are created equal.

'Now we are engaged in a great civil war, testing whether that nation, or any nation so conceived, and so dedicated, can long endure. We are met on a great battlefield of that war. We have come

to dedicate a portion of that field, as a final resting place for those who here gave their lives, that that nation might live. It is altogether fitting and proper that we should do this …

'It is rather for us to be here dedicated to the great task remaining before us – that from these honored dead we take increased devotion to that cause for which they here gave the last full measure of devotion – that we here highly resolve that these dead shall not have died in vain – that this nation, under God, shall have a new birth of freedom, and that government of the people, by the people, for the people, shall not perish from the earth.'

A month after Gettysburg, Wilkeson sent word to the Rookery that Lee had offered his resignation to President Davis. The South was under severe constraint but not yet on its knees. It continued to harass Northern forces. It continued to have success on the Georgia–Tennessee border and maintained control of the railroad center at Chattanooga until almost the end of November, when Grant burst its blockade. Lee put Burnside under siege at Knoxville, but Burnside held out. Lee's winning action at Cold Harbor turned out to be the Confederacy's last victory of the war.

A new chapter in blockade-running came to Washburn's notice when the *USS Kearsarge* reported sinking the Liverpool-built marauding cruiser *Alabama* on the French coast near Dieppe. What caught his attention was the tally of more than sixty merchant ships that the *Alabama* had either captured or sent to the bottom. In two years at sea she had diverted several Union ships from their blockading duties, forced insurance premiums to rise and caused many vessels to remain in port or seek foreign refuge. The more he heard about the *Alabama*'s exploits, the more the lawyer in Washburn speculated on a compensation claim against the neutral British government. He wondered, too, whether the *Trent* debacle and the supply of saltpeter had been resolved.

Washburn and Hill, stalking the Washington corridors and feeding the *Tribune*, detected a change of attitude in Greeley as 1864 wore on. The editor-in-chief was angered by military misfortunes that were turning the conflict into a bloodbath without end. He regarded Lincoln's leadership as mediocre, and feared defeat for the Republicans in November's presidential election if Lincoln was again their candidate.

In July the two *Tribune* men found themselves acting as go-betweens for Lincoln and Greeley in a clandestine peace proposal. Greeley discovered that a three-man mission from Richmond was standing by in Canada, empowered to talk peace with the Union. He implored Lincoln to accept the invitation because 'our bleeding, bankrupt almost dying country longs for peace'. He suggested four conditions, listing them as restoration of the Union, abolition of slavery, unqualified amnesty for secessionists and Federal payment of $400 million to former slave owners as compensation for their loss of property.

Lincoln asked Greeley to go to Niagara Falls to determine whether the emissaries were empowered to sue for a peace that would embrace an end to secession and abandonment of slavery. If their answer was 'yes', said the president, then bring them to the White House. Once at the Falls, Greeley was so intent on placing no impediment in the way of peace that he failed to mention the indispensable conditions. When the Southerners eventually learned of Lincoln's terms they claimed that their powers stopped at an informal exchange, and they issued a statement accusing Lincoln of going back on his word.

Thus ended any chance of talking peace. Washburn reckoned

that the true purpose of the Southerners was to influence Northerners opposed to the war at the coming polls. Acrimony broke out among the Northern press and politicians. The *Times* and the *Post* accused Greeley of being a cat's-paw in Southern treachery to undermine Lincoln, while Gordon Bennett's *Herald* branded him a nincompoop. The *Times* called for public disclosure of the texts between Lincoln and Greeley, to which Lincoln agreed if certain defeatist passages were taken out. Greeley agreed only if every word was included, and then turned down an invitation to the White House to thrash it out. His editorials in the *Tribune* lashed Lincoln over his alleged loss of a peace opportunity, and urged further initiative. Lincoln told his cabinet that Greeley was untruthful.

As talks foundered at the Falls, General Jubal Early's Rebel army advanced to within five miles of Washington before being repulsed. General Grant was experiencing a rocky baptism as the newly appointed commander of the Union armies until a real breakthrough occurred in August when Atlanta, the Confederacy's principal munitions depot, surrendered to General William Tecumseh Sherman. In November Sherman embarked on a 300-mile march through Georgia to the Atlantic coast. His troops lived off the land while cutting a sixty-mile-wide swathe of destruction, laying waste to railroads, factories, bridges and public buildings.

In the same month Abe Lincoln and George McClellan squared up for the presidential election. Greeley would have preferred the Free-Soiler Salmon P Chase or Frémont as the Republican candidate, but the thought of the Democrat McClellan in the White House was such an anathema that the *Tribune* editor swallowed hard and supported the incumbent wholeheartedly.

During the hustings Lincoln endangered his vote by refusing to sign the Wade-Davis Bill that required the electorate of each breakaway state to swear past and future loyalty to the Union before that state could be officially restored to the Union. His poll fears were unfounded, however. He was returned comfortably for a second term, with Andrew Johnson as his vice-president.

With Lincoln secure in the White House and Grant in charge of the army, the Union was headed for victory as the war approached its fifth year. In December Sherman captured Savannah and the Rebels lost Nashville. Union forces sealed off Wilmington, the last blockade-running port. Sherman undertook a march through the Carolinas. The Confederacy was short of food, and Lee's army began to leech away. A peace conference was proposed in the New Year that President Davis agreed to attend if recognition of Southern independence would be a prerequisite. This was unacceptable to Lincoln, and so the conference was never convened.

At the end of March, Lee's last gasp failed in two assaults on Grant's army at Petersburg. On 2 April the Old Gray Fox evacuated Richmond, and on 9 April he sat down with Grant at Appomattox Court House to agree terms.

News of the meeting gave the *Tribune* its last major scoop of the war from the pen of Henry Ebenezer Wing, a correspondent who made a splash in his buckskin jacket, Irish corduroy riding breeches, calfskin boots and kid gloves. Wing rivaled Washburn in ingenious ways of delivering reports of Fredericksburg, Cold Harbor and Gettysburg to the Rookery. At Appomattox he arranged for one of Grant's subordinates to signal a favorable outcome by mopping his forehead three times as the generals emerged from their talks. Wing reported that Lee's army was to be sent home on parole accompanied by their horses, with officers permitted to carry arms.

There was scarcely an intake of breath before politicians and press demanded recriminations, reciprocity, compensation or punishment. The *Tribune* cried out against the *Times's* call for Jefferson Davis to be hanged, arguing that such a fate would turn the Confederate leader into a hero and martyr. 'We plead,' Greeley wrote, 'against passion certain at this moment to be fierce and intolerant; but on our side are the Ages and the voice of History. We plead for the restoration of the Union, against a policy which would afford momentary gratification at the cost of years of perilous hate and bitterness.' His hope was that fellow citizens of Southern states would 'call out now for clemency and humanity toward former masters.'

Washburn and Hill were in almost constant touch with the White House to track the progress of peace, and Washburn composed a careful request for a transfer to New York that he considered for several days before submitting to Gay. He figured that it was timely to be at the nerve center of the paper if he was to realize his ambition to be an editor-at-large and commentator. He was fascinated with the new era of reconstruction and, particularly, the restored Union's relations with other nations. He learned that another Anglo-American attempt was to be made to lay a telegraph cable under the Atlantic that, if it succeeded, would change the way that news travels between continents. He also pondered, though not to Gay, on whether printing machines would soon be able to insert photogravure images and artists' depictions into newspapers on the night.

Politics apart, the end of hostilities brought about relief and rejoicing in Washington, and for Washburn a tingling note by his lover's hand via US Mail suggesting that she visit the capital because her Barnum tour was approaching its end in Baltimore. The time was approaching for the lovers to consider their future if he was to move to New York. Far more difficult for the relationship would be the news – only notional as yet – that the cable would carry him across the Atlantic.

For her visit to Washington, he reserved a suite at Willard's and bought tickets for a performance of Tom Taylor's farce *Our American Cousin* at Washington's finest drama center, Ford's Theater.

George and Ida were seated in a box adjacent to the stage, while President Lincoln and his family had equivalent seats across the auditorium. During the interval Washburn remarked to Ida that Abe was wearing the first smile he had seen in all his time in Washington. Just then a commotion broke out around the president when a loud report turned all eyes to see Lincoln slump under a puff of smoke. In a flash the intruder, gun in hand, leaped from box to stage and vanished behind the scenery.

Ida froze in her seat, and hissed, 'I recognize him ... that's John Wilkes Booth, the actor.' Washburn leaped up and rushed backstage to find that the would-be assassin had vanished into the night. When he returned to the auditorium, the wounded president had been borne to a house across the street.

Washburn's eye-witness account appeared in next morning's *Tribune,* and his follow-up later that day informed readers that while the alleged assassin, thought to be a Southern sympathizer, was on the run, the president had died of his injuries as dawn broke. Tears smudged his copy when he handed it in at the Rookery.

14

The Tribune sails to Europe

Wednesday, 1 August 1866, Atlantic Cable Office, London
Washburn's request to move to the editorial nerve center was answered by Gay amidst the turmoil of Lincoln's assassination and the death of Booth, his assassin, who was eventually hunted down in a burning barn by a Union soldier.

It was clear to the managing editor that his star of Antietam would be an admirable asset at the Rookery as the *Tribune* moved into a post-war era. Having attained good reporting, good writing and record circulation, and having seen most of the policies advocated in the paper come to fruition despite Greeley's rocky relationship with President Lincoln, the editor-in-chief and his staff must now confront how on earth to maintain the paper's momentum in peacetime. Gay reckoned that Washburn would be a valuable addition to the editorial nerve center in New York.

During the volatile political decade of the 1850s the *Tribune's* circulation had tripled to 55,000 copies daily. Such gains compared well with its upstart rivals, the *Times* sales being 35,000, the *Sun* printing 60,000 and the *Herald* 75,000 a day. During the same period, however, the *Tribune's* weekly edition that was distributed far and wide by rail quadrupled its circulation,

The apex of *Tribune* journalism before the war was the election of Abraham Lincoln to the presidency in 1860. During the conflict that followed, the stature of reporters was enhanced and reflected by changes in the paper's appearance. Advertisements were subordinated to news, and the concept of leading stories displaced chronological arrangement of editorial matter. The electric telegraph became the reporter's essential tool, while Hoe's invention of stereotyping, the etching of impressions of pages onto a cylinder that then printed them on continuous rolls of paper, enabled more papers to be produced faster. By the end of the war the *Weekly Tribune* was printing 200,000 copies and the total readership of the daily, weekly and Sunday editions was claimed to be 1.5 million. And this was achieved for much less than the $525,000 that the rival *Herald* spent on its war coverage.

By springtime in 1866, Greeley was devoting much of his time to his memoirs and no longer regarded the paper he founded as his personal instrument. His thoughts moved leftwards in politics to favor radical reconstruction of the South, and rightwards in business to favor less spending by President Andrew Johnson's new administration. He condemned Secretary of State Seward's proposal to purchase Alaska from Russia as absurd. His several attempts at electoral office failed, and at fifty-five his grandfatherly specs and cherubic features surrounded by his corona of white hair and whiskers indicated that he had outlived his time as an icon of homespun virtue.

Meanwhile, Sidney Gay, Greeley's second-in-command, had reached his fifties in declining health, and it was time for new blood. The youngest, most gifted and most flawed newcomer was John Russell Young. Lured from the Philadelphia *Press*, Young was a master of barbed characterization, once describing General Grant as a 'sashed and girded sphinx'. He wrote some pieces for the *Tribune* and ingratiated himself with Greeley. Now at the tender age of twenty-six he was appointed managing editor, much to the surprise of several on the editorial floor, including Washburn. Young introduced a military regime, disposed of dead wood, appointed his brother as chief of the Washington bureau and insisted on good timekeeping all round.

Young's talent was that he held a clear vision about the look and feel of the paper. He dropped the multi-deck headlines of the wartime front page for a more austere look while arranging stories in order of newsworthiness instead of chronologically. Advertisements continued to play second fiddle to editorial content.

He encouraged neat layout and typography and brought verve and energy to the paper's writing. He discouraged elaboration and encouraged more fact in what he called 'grocer's bill' style. Consequently his editorial page sparkled, and he allowed feature writers and correspondents wide stylistic latitude.

The new era was marked by the addition of a graphic tableau depicting the Spirit and Hope of United America that first appeared on the masthead on 10 April 1866. In its center was a clock set at 6.12 p.m., the time the first edition was due to roll. To its left a brooding Father Time, a ruined Greek temple, a man and ox with a plow, a camel train passing pyramids, and an hourglass. To the right was a Joan of Arc figure holding a billowing Old Glory banner, a railroad train, factories and smoking chimneys, a plow and a cogwheel. At the top an eagle is about to take flight.

Washburn soon felt at ease in the new regime on the editorial floor. He now possessed a thorough grasp of how the *Tribune* was produced, and he made foreign news, particularly European news, his fiefdom. He spent his days selecting the best stories sent in by correspondents and trawling through foreign papers as they arrived from the mail boat piers on the harbor.

Young walked up to his desk one morning waving a clipping from the London *Times* announcing that Prussia had declared war on Austria. 'I should like you to take the first steamer to London and find out what's going on in Europe,' said the managing editor. 'Coincidentally I received a letter from Karl Marx this morning,' placing a manuscript in front of Washburn, 'and ...'

'Karl Marx?'

'A journalist in London who apparently wrote frequently for us in the fifties. He describes a conversation with Dizzy Disraeli, the English Tory leader, who met von Bismarck a few years ago. Bismarck told Dizzy openly of his ambition to make mayhem in Europe by declaring war on Austria, subduing the minor German states, dissolving the German Confederation, whatever that is, and uniting Germany under Prussian leadership. Now he seems to be fulfilling his ambition.'

Two days later Washburn embarked from Boston aboard the *China*, the Cunard line's newest screw-propelled ship, bound for Liverpool via Halifax and Queenstown. *China* turned out to be but a knot slower than the *RMS Scotia,* holder of the Blue Riband for the Atlantic crossing. *China*'s low consumption of coal enabled her to carry more cargo than *Scotia.*

Washburn endured an anxious crossing. Although the latest in liners, the *China* was old-school height of luxury. The saloon had long benches for seats and racks of table glass overhead. The cabins were cramped and lit dimly by pungent, smoky oil lamps mounted in triangular cases that bisected two cabins. The sanitary arrangements were unspeakable.

The ship sailed up the east coast in atrocious weather and struggled to dock in Halifax for four hours, so fierce were waves and wind. On departing Nova Scotia, *China* was enveloped in fog that clung to the ocean as far as the Irish coast. The captain maintained fourteen knots, his top speed, causing Washburn to inquire if it was safe to sail day and night at such a pace in fog.

'Safe? Good God, no,' replied the captain.

'Then why do it?'

'For three reasons. First, I have to get to Queenstown and Liverpool in good time, or I will draw the ire of Mr Cunard. Secondly, fogs don't last forever, so the faster we go the sooner we will come into the light. Third, if there should be a collision, the vessel with the greatest speed comes off best.'

Washburn relayed this to a fellow passenger whom he recognized as Richard Henry Dana Jr, an experienced mariner who had written a best seller on the subject, *Two Years Before the Mast*.

'I like a captain to have the courage of his opinions, but not to tell his passengers,' Dana remarked. 'Keep it to yourself.'

Over the ensuing days the captain's third ' reason for undiminished speed was not put to the test. With nothing to see as *China* steamed ahead on calm gray waters, Washburn spent his time absorbing news from his bag of New York papers, and conversing with fellow passengers when the opportunity arose. One such was Dana who was keen to share entertaining episodes of his sailing days without revealing any fear of the captain's reckless navigation.

Then there was the occupant of Washburn's neighboring cabin, a quiet young man who spent his time sketching in the saloon. He turned out to be from Philadelphia on his way to take up a scholarship at the École des Beaux Arts in Paris. Having never seen more of Philly than the railroad depot, Washburn inquired if his book contained any city scenes, and to his pleasant surprise was shown a stream of depictions of boathouses and rowers on the Schuylkill River.

'I was raised on Mount Vernon Street near the water, and so I was soon messing about in boats. I learned to pull an oar and go rowing with my friends whenever we could.'

'Well, I don't blame you. You're fortunate to have some good water there by the look of it. I fell in love with rowing when I attended college at Yale, and when I moved to Boston I took every opportunity to get out on the Charles. I'm George Washburn, by the way, a scribe with the New York *Tribune*.'

'Pleased to meet you, Mr Washburn. I'm Thomas Eakins.'

The scribe and the sketcher henceforth swapped stories about rowing in New Haven, Boston and New York. Washburn regaled Eakins with tales of the Charles River where Harvard's crews, sons of brahmins and protestant old money identified by crimson silk headscarves, were often pitched against Irish immigrants from St Mary's Temperance Society, the Maid of Erin and Saint James Young Men's Catholic Total Abstinence Society.

Eakins described the lively boathouse scene on the Schuylkill by Fairmont Park, and gave Washburn a lesson on the pitfalls of depicting rowing on paper. 'I've studied life drawing at the Penn Academy of Fine Arts and anatomy at the Jefferson Medical School,' he said. 'The sort of slim boats we use make composing a picture difficult because they are so long and narrow, and then the light plays off water as well as the sky every few seconds, sparks and reflections and swirls from the oars ...'

'Rowing's not so easy to write about either,' Washburn said. 'If you are lucky enough to find a place where you can see a race, the action is usually a long way off and parallax plays hellfire with judgment.' He described his experience of the first Yale versus Harvard race, when Yale went down twice in the day to the Bostonians.

'I was captain, and so it still irritates me that were beat,' he said, 'but at least we started something. It all began because the new Boston, Concord and Montreal Railroad wanted to attract fares to Center Harbor resort on Lake Winnipesaukee in New Hampshire. We were naive. Between losing the first race and losing the second, we were plied with ale, mineral water and brandy, a hearty meal and cigars!'

He described matches off the battery between Whitehall ferrymen. 'There's plenty rowing in New York,' he said. 'There's regattas at Dunlap's Hotel on the East River and the Empire City club on the Harlem River. And sometimes by the Staten Island ferry, Nautilus Hall I think it's called. You've come across the Ward brothers? A foursome from up the Hudson Valley, unbeatable.'

Going through his newspapers one day, one item caught Washburn's attention. It gave notice that the proprietors of a private gymnasium on Sixth Avenue and Fourteenth Street intended to form a New York Athletic Club, modeled on such European institutions as the German Gymnasium near St Pancras railroad station in London. The pioneers were named as William Buckingham Curtis, Harry Buermeyer and John C Babcock. Surely, he thought, that must be the same Babcock who was architect, army scout, cartographer and oarsman? Washburn wondered to Eakins if Babcock had made any progress with his ideas of giving oarsmen seats that slide. Eakins was intrigued, saying he would mention it to his keen rowing friend Max Schmidt when he next wrote to him.

'Your friend Max might like to know of another experiment I happened upon,' Washburn said. 'I was visiting my parents in Troy on the Hudson, where my father's a pastor. I walked past a paper mill one day and spied a racing single as streamlined as a spear drawn up on the shore. Its keeper revealed that it was made of laminated paper, a process that he had discovered by accident when repairing a leak in Josh Ward's boat with materials to hand. He glued paper to the hull and sealed it with varnish. He figured, this Elijah Waters fellow, that a shell made entirely of paper with sealed air chambers for buoyancy would be stiffer and lighter than a Spanish cedar boat. This is the boat of future champions, he ventured. Something to look out for.'

All the while, fog persisted for day after day on the ship's passage until one morning a beach emerged some miles north of where the pilot of the *China* intended to be. He had to make a sharp turn to dock at Queenstown, the Irish port known to Bostonians as Cobh.

Once berthed, first up the gangplank was a small boy hollering 'All the news' all but invisible behind a vast stack of the day's *Cork Examiner*. Washburn was his first customer, giving him a wry smile and a big tip 'for enterprise, sonny'. His eye immediately caught news of the war:

Fourth of July, London: Prussian forces defeated Austria at Sadowa, known to the victors as Königgrätz. The Austrians are thought to be seeking immediate peace talks.

Washburn entrusted a note to Russell Young to the next mail boat to leave Queenstown for New York, informing the editor that the war was over before he could reach the battleground, but that he would call on Mr Dudley, the consul in Liverpool, before continuing to London. After briefly paying his respects to the consul he caught the London train in the company of Eakins, and the journalist and artist wished each other well in their enterprises and pledged to keep in touch with news of rowing. 'I don't know how keen the French are on aquatic sport,' Washburn said, 'but I hope you find somewhere to go rowing.'

'Well, Paris has the Seine and Marne running through it, so I expect to find some *aviron*.'

Washburn duly mailed details of the Austro-Prussian peace negotiations to the *Tribune* as they became available. An armistice between the antagonists was agreed on Sunday, 22 July, and under the title of Treaty of Prague, signed at Nicholsburg four days later. Then came the announcement Washburn had been waiting for, the real reason that Young sent him to London in the first place. On 27 July the steamship *Great Eastern* completed laying a telegraph cable under the Atlantic to connect Valentia, an island off the Irish coast, to Heart's Content in Newfoundland. The cable carried hopes that it would not break, as happened on previous attempts at joining the continents. On 29 July Queen Victoria sent the first message, addressed to President Johnson, and the cable opened for business.

On 1 August George Washburn walked into the cable office in London and handed a hand-written paragraph to the operator:

Dateline London, Wednesday 1 Aug 1866
Peace was certain at Berlin on Saturday. Bismarck and the king return this week. Prussia
carries all her points. The Liberals support Bismarck's foreign policy. Austria's naval
victory is much overrated. The Hyde Park riots and the movement to form exclusive Reform
League meetings have periled the Derby government.

His forty-nine-word report was the first news story to cross under the ocean by telegraph. It cost the *Tribune* $49 at a dollar per word.

When Washburn returned to the Rookery, he had witnessed the Prussian army on maneuver and filled several notebooks with the wisdom or otherwise of prominent British politicians, including the two leading rivals Disraeli and Gladstone. He had also quizzed the minister-president of Prussia, Otto von Bismarck, on his desire to merge the numerous German states. More than one observer in London suggested that seismic shocks to the map of Europe were on the cards if Otto has his way. The view from Whitehall and the 'fourth estate' in Fleet Street was that Prussia would challenge the old empires of Austria, Russia and France for influence, maybe dominance, over the heart of Europe.

Washburn's visit to London confirmed that the time was ripe to set up a *Tribune* bureau primed to pump news from Britain and what Britons referred to as the 'Continent' speedily beneath the Atlantic Ocean to American readers. The prospect was exciting, but how would Ida react to his permanent posting across the ocean? She had been pleased for his assignment to unravel what the Prussians and Austrians were up to. But what chance of her lighting up Europe with her talents? And how would *he* feel about that?

On 11 May 1867 a notice appeared in the New York *Tribune*. It said:

Mr Washburn sails for Europe today to act as foreign commissioner for the Tribune, resident in London.

Valentia to Heart's Content

If you enjoyed George Washburn's exploits In *News Fit To Print*, you may like its sequel, *Valentia to Heart's Content,* in which the former war correspondent is assigned to London as the *Tribune's* European Editor. His task is to set up a bureau to file hot news via cable under the Atlantic Ocean.

The cable that opened in 1866 linked the telegraph networks of two continents and transmitted messages in a couple of minutes. Before the cable was laid, print and mail voyaged under canvas or steam for up to two weeks to cross the ocean. Just as the Civil War created war correspondents, so the Atlantic cable gave birth to foreign correspondents.

Washburn settled in London and mixed with Fleet Street's great journalists, novelists and troublemakers. He covered the big stories such as Washington's massive claim for compensation from neutral Britain over failure to prevent the Confederacy's privateer *Alabama* leaving Birkenhead dockyard. He obtained exclusive interviews with Prime Minister Gladstone who desired Home Rule for Ireland and Prussian foreign minister Otto von Bismarck who was hell bent on enlarging Germany.

And he attended the biggest media event ever known when Harvard's rowing crew raced Oxford from Putney to Mortlake, and Washburn raced his fellow correspondents to be first to dispatch the result to America.

For extracts from Valentia to Heart's Content, register on heartheboatsing.com

Books by Christopher Dodd

Fifty years of writing about rowing has enabled Christopher Dodd to fill several volumes with its history and culture. *The Story of World Rowing* begins with Greeks, Vikings and Venetians and traces rowing's roots around the world. It explains Britain's influence in changing toiling at oars from a way of life into a sport. *Thor Nilsen* is the biography of World Rowing's first development director who spent fifty years spreading competitive and recreational rowing in Africa, Asia, South America, and the Olympic Games.

Unto the Tideway Born is the story of the watermen who work the River Thames and their Company that was founded in 1555. *Water Boiling Aft* is the history of London Rowing Club who's foundation introduced amateur rowing to the Tideway at Putney in 1856. *Bonnie Brave Boat Rowers* examines the lives of professional oarsmen and boat builders on the River Tyne, and relates how their feats were celebrated in Newcastle's nineteenth century music halls.

The University Boat Race and Henley Royal Regatta influenced the definition of the amateur and the rules of racing for rowing and other sports. The evidence is in Dodd's *Henley Royal Regatta, The Oxford and Cambridge Boat Race* and *Battle of the Blues* (with John Marks).

When it comes to world championships and the Olympics, *Pieces of Eight* records the blood and guts of the feisty British eight and their coach, Bob Janoušek, at the 1976 Montreal Games. *More Power*, a biography of Jurgen Grobler by Dodd and Hugh

Matheson, traces the life of the outstanding British coach who began training champions in East Germany.

For more history and journalism by Christopher Dodd see the blog heartheboatsing.com *and the magazine ROW-360.*